D1038353

FINCHY

by

Yolande Finch

WYNDHAM BOOKS
NEW YORK

Copyright © 1981 by Yolande Finch
All rights reserved
including the right of reproduction
in whole or in part in any form
Published by Wyndham Books
A Simon & Schuster Division of Gulf & Western Corporation
Simon & Schuster Building
Rockefeller Center
1230 Avenue of the Americas
New York, New York 10020

WYNDHAM and colophon are trademarks of Simon & Schuster
Designed by Eve Kirch
Manufactured in the United States of America

10 9 8 7 6 5 4 3 2 1

Library of Congress Cataloging in Publication Data

Finch, Yolande, date.
Finchy.

1. Finch, Peter, Sept. 28, 1916–1977 2. Actors—
Great Britain—Biography. I. Title.
PN2598.F44F56 791.43'028'0924 [B] 80-22853

ISBN 0–671–61008–2

FINCHY

I

THE TAXI SWAYED along the wet roads, winding through narrow streets, gray buildings melting into gray pavements carrying silent, slow-moving gray people. Horrible gray day.

Finchy's face stared down at us from the huge posters advertising his latest films, *Raid on Entebbe* and *Network*. In all his long career, I'd never seen him given such *star* publicity. I wondered if he was enjoying the attention way back there in dear old Hollywood. He hated Hollywood and always had. Perhaps he felt better about it now.

I looked at Charles, my son, our son. We had the same opinion of early mornings, so we hadn't spoken much since leaving the hotel.

"How do you feel, darling?" I asked him.

"Well, I'm not going to pass."

"Then we can all relax," I replied sarcastically.

"I'll do my best."

"I know you will, my love."

"It's the teaching I've been getting."

"Don't let's blame the teachers."

"I'll do my best."

"Well, that's the most any of us can do."

The rain hit the windows heavily and I peered out at still more posters of Finchy. It was incredible. They'd plastered the city with them. We'd have a good lunch and take in *Entebbe* this afternoon and *Network* tonight. I glanced at my watch. Seven-thirty. The driver lit up a Gauloise, releasing a lungful of smoke that engulfed us further.

"Is there some music on the radio?" I asked him, and watched him lean forward to turn the switch, concluding his action with a deep sigh.

"So gay, the French! So chatty. I love the way they brighten the day!"

"They're all right," responded Charles.

"I know, they're adorable. It's just that I don't understand them."

The voice of the announcer silenced us. President Giscard d'Estaing and his wife were giving a reception for some visiting political megalomaniac; more about La Belle France and her cleverness in all fields; the victims of the earthquake in Iran were of greater number than expected; South Africa . . . blah, blah, blah . . . I gazed sleepily at the cloudless morning, the slightly widening road as we left the center of town. "Peter Finch, the British actor, died last night in Hollywood, California."

What? *What?*

Charles and I looked at each other. What had the man said? He drew closer to me. We stared at each other. Had we heard something? Something to do with Daddy? Daddy dead? Silenced by the shock, we sat there, the announcement blanking us out as careening bolts of unspoken words tore between us. Huddling together, we waited for the full story. Was there a story? Had we misheard? Was it the earliness of the day . . . the strange city . . . the tension . . .? The utter impossibility! He couldn't die now! His posters were all over Paris! We were going to see him this afternoon. . . .

"Peter Finch, the British actor, collapsed at a news interview yesterday at the Beverly Hills Hotel, Hollywood. The distinguished actor, whose performance in his most recent picture, *Network,* has been highly praised throughout the world, is believed to have died last night. The cause of death was not immediately known, but it was believed to be a heart attack."

At last we could speak. What was there to say?

"He's dead!"

"The silly bugger. What a time to go."

"Mummy—Daddy's dead!"

"God, Jesus—if that isn't just like him. Oh God, what a fool!"

"I'll never pass the exam now." Good old Charlie. Right onto the positive aspect of what looked like a tragedy. I took him in my arms and looked into his face. No tears. Such a good boy, such a lovely, sweet-smelling, good-thinking, compassionate thirteen-year-old boy.

"I'm sorry, darling, my darling." I tried to cry.

"My God," said Charles, "he's dead! I've never met anyone who died before."

"The poor bastard. And in *Hollywood!* The place he hated the most. Poor old Finchy!"

The radio droned on with the rest of the world's worst news. I let it go. I'd have to think fast. Very fast. Samantha. What about Samantha? She was still back in Cannes. Of course she wouldn't be awake, not yet, but say she did get up and somebody had the news on? Say she hears before I can tell her? Oh God!

"What about Sammy?"

"I know, that's what I'm thinking. Oh my God—typical—just typical of him!"

"I hate him."

"No. Don't hate him, Charlie. It was never his fault."

The driver turned his ill-tempered face toward me and asked in his gruff, jarring voice where the school was.

"I told you," I replied. "It's the American school in St. Cloud."

"This *is* St. Cloud."

I stared at the long, wide avenue, so cold, so wet, so empty. Nothing there on either side looked like a school.

"You'll have to stop and ask."

"It's raining."

"Listen," I snapped, "my husband has just died and you're worrying about getting wet!"

His head whipped around. "Your husband?"

"Yes. My husband. If you were listening to the news, you would have heard that Peter Finch, the distinguished British actor, has passed away. In Hollywood, last night." Oh God, how degrading this was. I continued: "He was my husband and I have to get our son to the American school in St. Cloud for an exam, so for Christ's sake, find it!"

"Quelle horreur." His hands lifted off the wheel. That's right, I thought, kill us too.

"Je suis absolument dêsolê, madame."

"Thank you—now please."

"He was an excellent actor. Extra."

"That one cannot deny, monsieur. He was a great actor." I glimpsed Charles lifting his eyes to heaven.

It was now ten minutes to eight. We'd be driving along this endless avenue for an eternity. There was no school. There would be no exam, Peter was dead and all Samantha's dreams of growing up to be a great actress and walking onto a movie set one day to be introduced to him as his costar and then asking him, "Do you know who I really am?" . . . were gone . . . all gone. And Charles wanting, when he finally met his father again, to punch him first and then kiss him . . . All gone, too. Six years since I divorced him and he'd only seen them once. I had tried too hard, writing to him, keeping track of his whereabouts, hoping he'd come to them, forgive me and at least see his children. He had tried, too, in his own mad way, to find us, but none of us was there. I suddenly felt like vomiting . . . the guilt and the shame and now too late, too late to make peace.

"Darling," I said to Charles, "you don't have to take this exam. If you can't face it."

His hazel eyes, shaped so like Finchy's, gazed back at me, their expression very serious.

"No. I think I should."

"There it is, madame."

The huge white building that looked to me like a series of hangars stood back from the road. We studied it unhappily. What was the point?

"All right. Drop us there, please."

I doubted that the driver would charge less to the bereaved. I was right. I ladled out chunks of French francs and he waited for his tip, with hand extended and tears in his eyes. Disgusted, we made our way through the labyrinthian building and found the right room. Before releasing Charles, I whispered, "Don't worry about it. Under the circumstances, everyone will understand if you don't pass." I watched him disappear, then asked a jolly American matron where I could find some coffee. She directed me across the road to a workers' café, where I sat under the interested scrutiny of the early local drinkers . . . for the next two hours, the smell of piss and Pernod and the blue haze from black tobacco enveloped my senses and staved off the feelings of grief.

Sipping the greasy cognac, I thought of the previous night and the noises upstairs, those heavy, tormented footsteps. The walls and floors at that modest Left Bank hotel must be as thin as moths' wings, so close were those movements above my head. Or had I imagined them? Finchy was always hearing noises. Three knocks usually. "Christ! Did you hear that? Three knocks. There were three distinct knocks on the ceiling of this plane!" Always three knocks. Sometimes I wondered if the boy was a little unhinged. If there was a nun on the aircraft, we were in hell. "We're going to die, I tell you. A blackbird. I'll have to go up front. Can't stand it, Yo." One drink after that he'd be as pissed as a koala bear. Anything that frightened him got the alky to work faster, and flying was terrifying to Finchy. "Do you mind watching the engine while I take a leak?"

He was superstitious, but most actors are, with rabbit feet on their makeup tables, no whistling in dressing rooms, nothing green on stage and unmentionable titles of plays, curses and ghosts. Late at night, in bars, whispering things about the ides of March and keeping the spirits happy. All artists have a muse and they are very careful indeed not to anger her. She might, you know, just *might* put the squeeze on and that meant death.

Death! My mind wondered. Who was that man upstairs last night? When we'd left the hotel this morning, I had gently complained about the man in number 9, assuming that was the room that contained the night walker. The clerk had looked puzzled. "There's no one in that room, madame." I'd huffed disapprovingly. These French. Never admit to anything! I decided not to argue about it and also had a sudden, romantic flash of imagination that the clerk was hiding some escaped criminal. But now . . . If Finchy had died yesterday evening in Los Angeles, could he have been haunting us in the early hours? Ridiculous! And what an extraordinary way for Finchy to go. It wasn't like him. Or was it? He'd always said that when he left the building, he would go out number one. Had he left his Jamaican banana plantation and gone to Hollywood to become number one and die?

2

GOD KNOWS, Finchy had collected enough awards in his lifetime, but as far as awards are concerned, not many actors are too thrilled to receive them. Certainly, their price may go up on the market and they are a little something to hang up in the toilet (loo), but on the whole, these *memento mori* are not good luck and many actors curse them because so often they seem to keep the work away for the next twelve months. Finchy's distaste for them was well known. He had offended the Australians way back in 1946 when he'd used the statuettes awarded him for best actor of the year as a counterweight in the ball-cock system of the lavatory. I didn't know as I sat in that dreary café that day in January 1977 that Hollywood was going to present his dead body with the greatest award of them all, the Oscar. Poor old Finchy. I did know that he'd lived the life of a prince and a vagabond and perhaps even a rogue and that at last he had disappeared, and judging by the poem he read the evening before his death, may not have been as surprised as we were, because the poem went like this:

> Now I out walking
> The world desert,
> And my shoes and my stockings
> Do me no hurt.
>
> I leave behind
> Good friends in town

Let them get well-wined
And go lie down.

Don't think I leave
For the outer dark
Like Adam and Eve
Put out of the Park.

Forget the myth
There is no one I
Am put out with
Or put out by.

Unless I'm wrong
I but obey
The urge of a song:
I'm—bound—away!

And I may return
If dissatisfied
With what I learn
From having died.

"Away!" by Robert Frost

Finchy did his first disappearing act when he was in diapers. He was too young to be party to the intrigue that culminated in his being stolen from his pram in the first year of his life, but according to him, his mother's husband, Mr. George Ingle-Finch, suspected that the new addition to the family was not legit.

None of the major characters, excepting Ma, are alive now to verify or deny the rumor, tumbled and tossed over seas and continents, played down in private and played up by publicists, that Finchy was a bastard.

Had Mrs. Ingle-Finch succumbed to the charms of the dashing Major Campbell and had their efforts been rewarded by God with a son in the person of Finchy?

Ma, as Finchy fondly addressed his mother after rediscovering her thirty-five years later, was not saying and Ingle-Finch had long since passed away, but Major Campbell, whom fate tossed at me in Moffat, Dumfries, in 1970, swore he was Finchy's father, and he didn't have to swear very much; they were the spitting image of each other.

Dodging the issue himself, Finchy stayed well out of reach of either man.

George Ingle-Finch was a famous explorer and mountain climber and a notorious shit. Enraged by his wife's infidelity, he snatched Finchy from his pram and took him to live in France with his unmarried sister, a cult figure in a circle of followers of Eastern philosophy.

There, immersed in the words and wisdom of Buddha, he grew up, among the great and not-so-great who visited his aunt's salon in Vaucresson, a small town outside Paris. Nijinsky and Isadora Duncan were members of this clique, which believed in and studied the life of Buddha. Keen to discover the meaning of life as he had, they tried to emulate the hunger and poverty that seemed to bring with it the eternal peace they craved. Every year, these fashionable acolytes traveled to India, elegantly dressed in saffron robes and carrying begging bowls, and blindly followed their gurus. Finchy was right along with them, shaven head, begging bowl and all. He was only seven years old.

It surprised me that he never went back to India, for he remained a fringe Buddhist throughout his life, and even during the war he never fired a shot. Not quite a vegetarian, he righteously avoided red meat, preferring a quiet Harrods sausage or my homemade cottage pie. They didn't look like any animal he'd ever seen, he said. A great dissembler was old Finchy.

Vaucresson, a typical, small, bourgeoise town, afforded Finchy several years of near-normal life. The photos of him then portray a handsome boy of serious countenance, but with an unmistakable query in his eyes. Where was Mama? Or conceivably, who was Papa?

He went to the local school in his black *tablier,* a sort of pinafore with a big black bow at the neck, and wore sabots on his feet. His French was always perfect and until forty years later, when he contracted some nasty disease from the polluted seas of the French Mediterranean, he remained a Francophile.

He took me to Vaucresson to show me his aunt's home and the neighboring mansion wherein his first loved had lived. With that young Colette or Suzanne—her name escapes me now—he had discovered the excitements and pleasures of sex under the branches of the giant mulberry tree that now stood so forlornly in the garden, waiting, perhaps, for the young lovers to come back.

We couldn't get by the padlocked gate, so we stood with our faces pressed to the tall iron fence, imbedding lines in our skin and trying to see the ghosts of the young lovers. Many girls had lain under Finchy in the next thirty-five years and I was the latest, but I remember feeling very close to him for wanting me to share that memory with him.

When Finchy was ten, his dreaded guardian, Ingle-Finch, discovered that the religious activities of his sister and her playmates included the practice of free love and homosexuality, albeit in the most sophisticated way, and decided that Oriental eccentricities may be all right for some people, but his "son" would be better off in the healthy atmosphere of Australia under the guidance of George's elderly father.

To be parted from a kindly, if unusual, aunt and his first love must have shattered Finchy, but parted he was, and with a trunk twice his size, he boarded a cargo steamship for Australia under the captain's charge. He was always somebody's charge.

George Ingle-Finch, Sr., was well into his eighties when the young Finchy stepped onto Australian soil for the first time. Ingle-Finch and his sister, a spinster lady only slightly younger than himself, took the child to their hearts. To hear Peter speak, George Sr. was the only man on earth that he had ever loved or trusted. For the first time in his life, he became the center and pivot of a real, if small, family.

The old couple grew vegetables in their back garden and there was even an orchard where Finchy could play Tarzan. The sun shone brightly and hotter than in Vaucresson; he learned to swim and he made his first "mates" at Sydney High School. Free from the compulsive single-mindedness of French education, he flourished in the more relaxed atmosphere of his new country.

It must have been a great adjustment for the old pair, but it seems there was nothing that marred their happiness with their "grandson" except for the existence of two pet blackbirds, well installed in the affections of the old man. Sitting on each of his shoulders, they glared at the newcomer with suspicion. Finchy glared back. The pattern was struck and the battle was on.

Old George innocently played his affection to all three with an open hand, but now that Finchy had at last found the one man he needed to love, he needed that man to love him more than he loved those stupid birds.

The murder that was in his heart soon manifested itself. At twelve years old, Finchy hit out in a rage at one of the birds when it dive-bombed him. Horrified, he carried the corpse away and buried it under the wooden substructure of the house.

"The bloody thing flew straight at me. I was trying to get it away from my eyes! I thought it was attacking me. I bloody *knew* it was attacking me."

Forty-five years later Finchy would wake gasping with fear as the nightmare of his childhood guilt terrorized his dreams.

"Grandfather kept looking for it. For weeks he called out for the bloody thing. I felt like a murderer and I couldn't tell him. I never told him and I'm only telling you so that I can try to forget about the whole bloody episode. Bloody birds. They give me the creeps!"

So when the fear of death caught him while he slept beside me and he came back gasping and crying "death," that was the dream and the shock and the guilt of it. It took him seven years to tell me, and once he had spoken it out, the nightmare was exorcised.

Finchy had four years with the old couple before the sister died. Her brother soon followed her. Finchy was alone again and life was not going to get easier. Later he often quoted an old Arabic expression: "Life," he would say, "is like a cucumber. It's either in your hand or up your ass." From the moment George went to heaven, the cucumber was up Finchy's ass.

They say there is some good in everyone, but from the description of his next human bus-stop, that lady was close to the exception. Shuttled after George's funeral to Ingle-Finch's other sister, he became, at fourteen, the victim of a depressive sadist whose humiliations and cruelty upon him were so intolerable that, rather than suffer further, he took to the streets. He was slugged out of bed at four in the morning to clean and scrub, he was starved and beaten and ripped apart by kitchen knives. He described how the woman forced him to eat his own excrement. A magnificent scar ran up from the inside wrist of his right arm to his elbow, and Finchy, with wry humor and even a little pride, offered it for inspection to many interested friends when he grew up.

He never dwelt long on this terrifying patch of his past, preferring for the sake of survival to push it far back into his already deeply wounded psyche. But when he lifted his sleeve and pushed forward his arm for viewing, it seemed to me he was saying: "If I could come through that one, I can come through any of the other shit they want to hand out!"

Finchy's life moved with the unnerving disorder of a Mexican jumping bean. From one year to the next, he never knew how or where destiny was planning to lay down his path.

So, being an intelligent man, he discarded the comforts of furniture and wardrobe, photos in frames, and even books. Although he was a voracious reader, I never saw him buy a book. They seemed to appear in his hands from friends and publishers, and there they stayed, by his side, ever ready for his probing.

A small pack of favorites somehow always remained with him, gathering dust and endearing rings of coffee cups or the dried trickle of red wine, particularly his "Sheats and Kelley," the English poets whose names he had turned to his own liking.

He could quote "Ode to a Grecian Urn" without a break and through any catastrophe. T. S. Eliot's *Waste Land* spurted from him on the prow of some furious embattled banana boat in mid-

Atlantic and he was always on some banana boat in mid-Atlantic in the worst season. The sonnets of Shakespeare hushed and roared from his throat on happy drunken nights; Othello's love poems to Desdemona warmed me often and made us cry as I lay in his arms. Hamlet was there and Chaucer and Donne, rendered beautifully and with great loving concentration. What an actor he was.

Finchy loved "the word" that transmits man's emotions, but he himself rarely attempted to create his own poetry, choosing, like most actors, the humbler role of putting the breath of life into another man's.

"In the beginning"—he would smile—"there was 'the word.' " The fact that "the word" was *logos* or reason was irrelevant, because there was very little "reason" in Finchy's nature. Only nature mattered, and feelings and mysteries and infinity. So he preached, pissed or sober: "We, my love, are finite. We must not question the infinite."

He was way beyond me. But I would have liked to know some of the answers.

3

FINCHY WAS A LEGEND in his lifetime, and mostly for raising hell. But in 1977, Hollywood awarded him the Oscar. And Hollywood gave it to an actor who couldn't do anything more for Hollywood.

The Oscar was awarded posthumously. The movie was *Network* and Finchy played the mad broadcaster as if he was never going to get another chance at the game. Into that performance went the uncanny magic that was the essence of the man himself. That performance brought him almost every award the film industry had to offer. He had made it, just as he'd always said he would. "When I go, I'm going out number one."

But that really was not like Finchy. One of his greatest charms was his modesty, especially with regard to his work. He'd given great performances before, in *Sunday Bloody Sunday, Oscar Wilde, The Nun's Story,* and he'd never shown any signs of being self-satisfied. If anything, he was too much the retiring violet. Praise embarrassed him and he never, never discussed his craft. It was taboo to meddle about with his muse, his true mistress.

His public image, though, was no myth. He was a pisspot and a hell raiser, but he was also a happy drunk, a gigglebum and very, very good company. He was handsome, with a great dignified head; wide, deep blue eyes whose corneas were ringed with black; a bone structure that defied a bad angle, with cheekbones as high as an American Red Indian's with deep hollows beneath; and a pursed, sensual mouth I have heard ladies describe as "bee-stung!" His hair was curly and the color Vivien Leigh gave it, baby elephant. He was tall enough at just under six feet, had broad shoulders and rangy hips and was not vain. Perhaps the most beautiful part of him was his hands, which were as long and slender and tapered, like blades of grass, into fine sculptured fingers with pale oval nails. They could be very tender hands and he used them when he talked, like an extra language or like an Italian aristocrat.

For a beach bum from Australia, Finchy had a lot of class, more class than he liked to admit. He was always pretending he wanted to be one of the people, whatever that meant, but his very complexities and contradictions, his very past, precluded that idea.

His "mateship" was a sort of cover, a way of pulling the wool over everyone's eyes, being one of the boys. There was a time in his life when he had to be one of the boys, back in the bad old days of the Depression. Everyone who had nothing in those days was one of the boys and that's how they survived. Back in 1933 when Finchy had plunged out of the horror that was life with the mad aunt, he was on the streets with nowhere to go and nothing to eat. For once, Fate was kind. He joined the vagabonds, living with men who had no homes or families or jobs. Compared to what he had just escaped, life was a bowl of cherries, although, as he would say, "It was some bowl of fucking cherries!" He made friends, though, men who called one another "mate," a term of affection he continued to use all his life. He stole food and booze and was always hungry. The alcohol filled the empty spaces inside and the friendships were strong and protective. One day he was so hungry—so hungry, he told me—that he could have eaten a baby's asshole through a wicker chair, and he and a mate stole a few goldfish from a bowl someone had foolishly left on a windowsill. They cooked the five little fishes over a camp fire and had goldfish sandwiches for tea. He said it was the nastiest taste he had ever experienced. "Never have a goldfish sandwich, mate," he warned me. "It's the most disgusting meal in the world!"

Around the cities, life got tougher and tougher and eventually Finchy moved "upcountry." He tried his hand at being a jackaroo, an apprentice on a sheep farm, and loved the life: riding the boundaries of the giant estates, sleeping under the eucalyptus trees with his head on the saddle, a blanket over him and a billycan beside him. What more could a man want?

Sheepshearing was another trade Finchy picked up on the outback, although the violence of the work never appealed to him, and the idea of getting that close to another animal's testicles with a shearer petrified him. Finchy was terribly ball-conscious. When he laughed, he would bend over holding his hands around his as if they might burst in their own happy appreciation. And at the first sight of a nun, he would clasp them with all his might. To reminisce accurately, it went like this: For one nun, he would touch them, for two, take hold and for three, clasp them with all his might. From what ancient superstition stemmed this habit (pun), I'll never know.

After three years as a jackaroo, he headed back for Sydney with a little money in his pocket and a lot of living under his belt. He got a job on the Sydney *Herald* as a cub reporter, and the boy had landed on his feet. Life began in earnest. He was as free as a bird and yet part of a profession that made sense and was dramatic.

He made his best friends in those years as a budding journalist, and all his life his relationships with reporters were good. He was straight with them and when he didn't want them to print something, he'd hold up his hands, pointing his index fingers upward to indicate, "Don't quote me, fellas." I don't think any of them let him down.

He told me one hilarious story about the death and burial of a much loved elder member of the Sydney Press Club. Old McKay never denied himself the pleasures of the bottle, but old age was catching up with him, and his taste for the strong stuff was doing nothing to delay his departure from this earth. He resisted the inevitable hospital until the very end, but the very end was at hand and he was dragged off to one for his last few weeks. His mates at the club were deeply troubled and Finchy promised to bring him a volume of John Donne, but never quite made it. McKay died. The old journalist had made his mates swear to let his ashes rest in one or other of the two places he loved most, the Sydney Press Club, preferably behind the bar, or his beloved Sydney Harbor, as second choice. Weepily, they promised to accede to his wishes and after the cremation interred his ashes in an old tobacco tin and solemnly placed it behind the bar among the bottles so beloved of their dear departed friend. Soon, however, the presence of the silent silver tin glaring at the drinkers became oppressive, a sort of reminder of what they were doing to their livers, and the boys decided to remove him to his second choice for resting place.

In company of the old tobacco tin that had become too hard to live with, a dozen or so of the fellas, including Finchy, who was still smarting with the guilt at not having produced John Donne, solemnly made their way down to the harbor and boarded a rowboat. Pissed out of their skulls, they rowed out to sea. Each man sent up a homage as distinctly as their condition permitted and the tin box was dropped into the ocean. The men turned the boat around and made to set back to land—they needed a drink. Glancing about to be sure their departed mate had settled nicely into his watery grave, the chaps were appalled to see the box bobbing up and down on top of the waves. They rowed back and gently tried to push the vessel under the water. McKay wasn't having it. After a frustrating half hour, patience was running out.

"Go on, get down, you bastard!" shouted one old friend, giving the box a vicious shove. The box bounced back.

"Down, you silly old fart," said another. McKay wasn't playing. The sun was sinking and McKay was going to stay afloat.

"Stupid fucker," shouted Finchy, and landed a brute of a whack on the box.

"Under, you cunt," screamed the mates. All on their feet now, the journalists pounded and belted the tin with everything they had.

"He won't go, the stupid asshole," and, "Git under, you old bugger."

"Wot a tit!" and so on, until in disgust they rowed back to

shore, the moon bright on their heads and their old matey floating behind them as safe as any man can be.

"If I ever decide to be buried at sea," said Finchy to me years later, "for Christ's sake, remember to open the bloody tin. They're a bastard to sink!"

By now he had moved on from journalism into the fringes of show business. He was becoming the advertising voice of Australia and enjoying at the same time a career in soap operas, for which that country was famous. They needed radio in that immense country. With his deep, sympathetic voice, he soon became the invisible answer to Gary Cooper, Australian accent or no. The work was a piece of cake—good money, easy hours, and pretty girls. He now had the time to pursue his only real hobby, being a beach bum. Hours each day were spent sunning around pools and beaches. Old Snake Hips, as he was known, was not short of admirers.

4

FINCHY FOUND his first wife on the beach. He found me on a beach, too, but I don't know what that signifies. He found his third wife in Jamaica and that's got a lot of beaches, so one can only surmise.

Tamara was dark-haired and pretty and, like Finchy, young. She was a dancer with the Diaghilev ballet, whose world tour was interrupted by the outbreak of World War II. Tamara and her mother decided to stay on in Australia, although that continent was getting edgy about the possibility of being attacked by the Japanese, but Europe was well into the war, and so Australia must have seemed the safer choice. Tamara and Finchy married after a whirlwind romance and although Finchy still held strongly to his Buddhist pacifism, all the boys were joining up, so, reluctantly, he did too.

He chose, for some reason that still puzzled him years later, the gunners. Skinny as a nail, with his legs half encased in flapping khaki shorts, his ribby chest hidden by an oversized balloon of a shirt, and most of his face covered by the cavalierish Aussie hat with its chin strap hooking it onto his head, he looked so defenseless that his mates referred to him sarcastically as the "Flower of Australian Manhood."

"They'll just laugh when they see you, mate. Those Jappie buggers'll laugh their yellow knockers off, you stupid bastard."

Little did his unit know they weren't off to protect the far end of their own country but were headed out over the seas to the Middle East with all the other poor sods. One day Tamara found herself waving from the quay, a war bride, as the ship left, taking her new husband with it. He was away for the duration of the Australian commitment.

The war only convinced Finchy further that he would have been better locked up as a pacifist. It appalled him. The waste of life, the boredom, the mad muddle of it all. He sat, dazed by the heat, behind his artillery gun, and never fired a shot. He never even got close to a German. The boys began to think someone had invented the Huns: "'Oo is this bleedin' 'Itler? It's a joke, mate! Wot a load of old cobblers . . . ," and so on and so on.

As for the healthy sexual appetites of the thousands of fellows in the ranks, most of whom had hardly discovered what their secret weapons were for, the army generously provided a couple of Arab whores in a tent.

"Can you imagine it? Three hundred guys queueing in the scorch for a quick poke? I was so randy by the time my chance came, I thought I'd be up her like a rat up a rope, but I couldn't make it. Me thing had gone dead. The thought of going into the poor bitch after all those guys killed it stone dead. I was bloody impotent. The sodding bastards had strangled me prick."

Finchy was still impotent when he got back to Tamara, although he must have made it once, because she produced a daughter, Anita, but after that, as he put it, it was always "Maybe Tamara, Tamara, Tamara, Tamara . . . ," but he couldn't get back his manhood. He began to drink heavily, hoping to revive the poor dead zone.

As a family, they lived together with Tamara's mother, a stern Russian Babushka who didn't approve of Finchy in the first place, thinking he wasn't good enough for her daughter. She bullied him and made him feel uncomfortable when he took one too many, so Finchy started "fighting" with his hat, and that meant leaving. He discovered in his search for more congenial company a dainty little half-caste hooker with a heart of gold. Finchy moved in with her and she brought him back to life. The half-caste Australian girls are considered the most beautiful of all the women on the continent and she loved him, and boy, did he need her! I'm glad he found her, because many years later I needed someone like that myself, but they aren't around for women.

I've often thought that Finchy's well-known penchant for the black women in his later life was his way of trying to recapture what must have been a very happy time.

Certainly, whenever he felt threatened sexually, he would dive off to somewhere he called "the wild wet woods," under London, into dark, noisy black clubs where he could feel less afraid. He himself called this "his need for the gutter"—"I have to rub my face in the dirt, Yo. Need it." This compulsive gutter search that debased him, was to have a devastating effect on us, and even now I'm not sure I really understand it, but I feel that somehow Finchy believed that a black woman would magically revive his "pork sword," as he referred to it. To me, the tireless erection is a sign of some nervous obsession that has very little to do with sex. Sex for ego maybe, but not sex for pleasure.

Having sorted out this important personal problem, the veteran decided not to go back into radio, but to extend his horizon by putting together a company of players who would tour the country taking the great plays out to the people.

He started by capturing his unwilling public—a little as Nero did in Rome when he locked the door of the theater until he had finished his performance of poetry reading and drama—by playing to them at their factories or places of work. It took courage to ask the ordinary beer-swilling Aussie male to sit still and listen to Molière, but with a dedication and perseverance that were much stronger in him than most people realized, he made a go of it.

He wanted the people to have a share of the greatest works created by man for man. He must have fought like hell, but his efforts bore fruit, for after a few years his company became so popular that the national conglomerate that controlled entertainment in Australia tried to put him out of business. Always a good sign. He became famous.

When the brilliant Old Vic Company visited Australia under Laurence Olivier and his wife, Vivien Leigh, they were brought to a performance Finchy and his company were giving at a factory during the lunch break. He was presented to the famous couple, who then watched the show. The Oliviers were impressed.

"If you ever come to England," said Olivier, "get in touch. You're good."

England was a long way away and he had a family. How was he going to make it?

That meeting was to be very important in more ways than one. He had met the greatest actor in the world and he had met the woman who was to be his greatest passion, his mistress and very nearly the death of him. Vivien Leigh had a lusty appetite for young actors and I imagine the electricity sparked her and Finchy off at that first handshake.

But first things first. He needed the patronage of Larry Olivier and somehow he was going to have to answer the knock of opportunity.

He started saving for the trip to England, "and it wasn't sparrow shit either, mate, I can tell you." He'd have to slave to buy berths for the four of them, Babushka, a widow, included. At last they could leave.

The trip took six weeks and everybody, except Finchy, was as sick as a dog. He was never sick on boats. He was never sick.

They settled into a cheap flat in Nottinghill Gate and Finchy started the heartbreaking calls to Olivier. "Nothing at the moment, old son. Call again."

After six months the family was penniless. Finchy started taking odd jobs, delivering newspapers and washing dishes. Usual old thing for starvers, but he was starting to panic.

"It ain't easy for an unheard-of actor from the bleedin' outback to find work on the London stage. I was thinking of getting the hell out of it and going home. No city is fun to be skint in. Back there I was a star, but in London I was just some digger—a freak."

At last the call came. Larry hadn't forgotten.

"We're doing a play called *Daphne Laureola.* There's a part in it for a young man, the Polish lover. If you get it, you'll be playing with a very great actress, Edith Evans. Would you like to audition?"

His chance had come and he took it like the man he was, ambitious, full of talent and determination.

His powerful audition got him the part. Maybe then, he felt like the man who only had two things in his briefcase, a sandwich and a revolver. Now, at least, he didn't need the revolver.

Completely unknown, he stepped into stardom and never glanced back. Not that I think Finchy would have accepted failure for his adult life. He had had enough of that as a child. No, he was going to make it and he did, swearing then that they were never going to get him alive and when he went, he was going out . . . well, we know which way he went out.

The critics praised him, and the audiences adored him. Edith Evans was a superlative actress and one of history's greatest comedy performers. Finchy worshiped her and says he fell in love with her. Never a beautiful woman in anyone's furthest imagination, Edith Evans had the magical gift of surrounding herself with an aura of beauty. Her look, her walk, the way she moved her arms, created about her almost an ectoplasm of exquisite femaleness.

She made herself beautiful. Rather in the same way as another great thespian, John Barrymore, at the age of eighty, could fool people that he was in his prime, a blindingly handsome man of thirty-five.

Errol Flynn, a great mate of Finchy's, told Finchy about how one night long ago in Hollywood, when Stars kept bungalows at the Garden of Allah off Sunset Boulevard, he heard a knock on his door. Upon opening it, he encountered a shriveled figure wrapped in a black cape, the head dropped onto the chest. Startled, Flynn told the figure to make itself scarce.

"Let me in," said an old voice, "I just want to relieve myself."

"Who are you?" persisted Flynn.

"Barrymore, boy. Barrymore," replied the dreadful vision.

"Of course, sir, please come in," and Errol quickly admitted the man, deeply impressed that the greatest should come calling on a simple up-and-coming actor—although notorious already for his way with both the women and the bottle.

Once inside, the horrible apparition crept toward the fireplace, undid his fly and relieved himself then and there. Flynn was not amused, but when the famous face turned toward him with a slightly wicked smile and held out a claw for a drink, Errol submitted. Hero worship dies hard in actors. God, thought Errol, how old he is!

Some time later and after a few jars, Barrymore suddenly addressed himself to the young actor.

"No, my son, I'm not really that old. Watch this."

With his two hands clasped under his chin, Barrymore began to pull an invisible mask from his face. Very slowly, as if the old skin dragged and stung, he pulled upward over his chin and nose and eyes and forehead and at last flung the cursed invisible thing away from him. As he straightened his body, he lifted his shoulders and his head and there, miraculously, stood a man of six feet three, a young man of six feet three, with such an amazing power in his eyes that poor old Errol nearly fainted with fear. Barrymore had become his youth, his shining blinding youth, and right in front of the amazed young Errol Flynn. Such is the way a great artist can fool not only himself, but the millions too.

Apart from her very special way of appearing beautiful when she decidedly was not, Evans played laughs as though she'd invented the ideas. Her secret, she explained to the dazzled Finchy, was this: "Comedy dear, is just like blowing powder puffs out of a cannon!" This made Finchy very aware of how much he had to learn, although comedy never became his forte. Later, *Simon and Laura* with Kay Kendall proved an unhappy excursion into comedy. He never had the wit. That delicate touch he had with tragedy, though, could very well have been learned from Edith Evans.

During the first months of his success in *Daphne Laureola,* when he was finding his feet and many new friends in the theater, he was called to the telephone backstage during intermission. Of course he was used by now to getting calls from admirers.

"Hello?"

"My name is Betty Stavely-Hill." The voice sounded young and interesting.

"Yes?" Finchy answered eagerly.

"Are you Peter Finch?" Such an interesting, well-bred, feminine voice.

"Yes. Yes I am." Finchy was warming. "Why?"

There was a silence. Finchy was intrigued. "Are you there?" he asked.

"Peter." Pause. "Peter, I think you are my son."

"What?"

"My son. I thought you were dead."

5

ALTHOUGH I PREFER to reverse the happy quote into "Time wounds all heals," it seems that Finchy forgave his mother and clung to his long-lost Ma with devotion, although this magnificent obsession had an ambivalence within that caught all women, including me, unawares.

The conflict broke down easily into two forms of behavior. One, he worshiped her and tried to recapture those lost years at breast and knee, and two, he reverted to infantile behavior like a bear slipping into warm molasses. He sulked, was naughty, ran away and came back, slept on the floor by her bed, brought the wrong girls home and put Ma through a right old love-you/hate-you dance from the moment she found him until the day he died. They had found each other after thirty-five years, but perhaps thirty-five years was too late. She paid high.

Another reaction to his latent Oedipal chagrin was his misted view of women in general, idolizing them at one moment and trampling them into the mud the next. His deep distrust of the female of the species was directly attributable to Ma, as was his intensely suspicious nature and his Rabelaisian possessiveness.

A subtle mystery surrounded their relationship, in my opinion, certainly by the time I came into the picture, and I would have liked to know some of the answers. Had he ever asked his Ma what had actually happened when he disappeared all those years ago? How had she reacted as a mother? Had she fainted from shock? Collapsed with grief? Called in the police or just accepted the abnormal, not to say criminal, act of her betrayed husband and settled for the punishment? I was never to know and I doubt Finchy knew either.

"Ma" had a mews house in Chelsea. She had divorced her last husband and now lived with her daughter from that marriage, Flavia, and presented Finchy to his own older brother, Michael, who he hadn't known existed. Finchy's cup flowed over. He was among his own family once more and it didn't seem to matter that he had suffered terribly on the long and lonely journey.

His own marriage was getting bumpy. Success was gorgeous; he had the world on a string. The muscles of his ego were beginning to flex. He joined the other actors from West End productions who gathered at the Salisbury, a famous pub in St. Martin's Lane, to unwind after the show.

Richard Burton was coming up at the Old Vic and was every actress's dream male. There was Claire Bloom; Maxine Audley and Kay Kendall, the funny and beautiful woman whose early death stunned show business; Robert Shaw and dozens of other hopefuls. The Royal Academy of Dramatic Art was at its peak, presenting the *crème de la crème* of its graduates to the profession: Peter O'Toole, Tom Courtenay, Albert Finney were to burst out of RADA in just a short while. Sean Connery was delivering milk in Edinburgh, and Michael Caine was carrying fish around Billingsgate, but their proletarian chores were to be interrupted by stardom.

Finchy started his affair with Vivien in earnest. Leigh, a convent-educated and exquisitely beautiful woman, but unfortunately cursed with a disturbing tendency toward alternating mania and depression, found in the young Australian actor, not only an amazing virility, but also a character that was sweet, modest and tender.

Her illness was still in its earlier stages, her periods of madness infrequent and still under control. As consort to the King, Olivier, she was a woman to be envied and undoubtably desired. Her husband, in all his wisdom, might have turned a blind eye to her peccadilloes.

Never as great an actor as Olivier, she worked tirelessly in her efforts to match his brilliance. He certainly gave her the opportunity to prove herself in the many great parts she played beside him; but the critics never gave her the credit she felt she deserved. Some say that it was partly this obsession to equal Olivier that aggravated her already developing madness. To Finchy, however, she was an angel incarnate, and the devil inside her was extra spice.

At this time, Finchy did not appear to be an alcoholic. He drank for fun and to be sociable. It was one way of not going home, or something to do while he waited for Vivien's call. He was a night man and a man of many faces. One never knew with Finchy, when one met him, whom exactly he was playing. Sometimes it was the intellectual, sidling along Charing Cross with his nose against the panes of bookshops; sometimes he was the melancholic romantic like Byron and sometimes he would entertain the drinkers, usually at Jacks, with some dreaded Australian doggerel:

> When lopin' in yer saddle
> At yer side a billycan
> And the lazy moon is hanging [long pause] up above!

These Aussie poems went on interminably and were recited with great feeling: ". . . with the great moon hanging"—longer pause and finger pointed upward—"up above!" They bored everyone shitless, but mercifully the mood only took him every few weeks, and drunk enough, one can see something romantic and sentimental about some poor bloke loping along in his saddle, at his side a billycan and the lazy moon . . . sniff . . . hanging . . . up . . . above. Enough to make anyone cry.

Following these maudlin sessions, Finchy would ring up his friends the following day and ask:

"Was I recitin' poetry? I'm very, very sorry."

The singing of "Waltzing Matilda" was not allowed.

Finchy had taken over from Dirk Bogarde, already a successful screen actor, in *Point of Departure,* with Mai Zetterling, at the Duke of York's. In a few years he wouldn't have to take over from anyone. He appeared in other Olivier productions including *Othello,* in which he played Iago opposite Orson Welles. His British film career started promisingly with the prisoner-of-war picture *The Wooden Horse,* and *The Miniver Story,* and J. Arthur Rank gave him a contract. That inevitably meant taking the good with the bad—"I gave them my 'Look, no. A19 today' "—but he got a chance at some distinguished pictures, including Graham Greene's *The Heart of the Matter,* and *Father Brown.* Later he did a cinema version of Nevil Shute's *A Town Like Alice* in Australia, where he decided they didn't appreciate the personal success he was having in the Mother Country, as it was called then. He'd been away in London for ten years and the Australians would still greet him with "Ain't sin you around for a bit, digger. Where you bin, mate? Exploring the outback?" He didn't care for that.

Vivien, who had had her glorious success as Scarlett O'Hara in 1939 (to her fury she hadn't been chosen to play opposite Olivier in *Wuthering Heights* the same year—Merle Oberon beat her to it) had been contracted to *Elephant Walk,* to play the glamorous, dissatisfied wife of a drunken polo-playing plantation millionaire in India. Typical old American milk-bar type of movie, with a young, equally glamorous younger male stud required to beef up the boring theme as "the love interest." Finchy was chosen to play the character and not without, one suspects, a little help from the woman who was to all intents and purposes his mistress. Not for one moment would I insinuate that Finchy was on the make, that he was any kind of gigolo, but, as he loved Vivien and she needed him as support, the scheme appeared foolproof—always a bad sign.

At this stage, "the wild wet woods," the mystical gutters that enticed Finchy on his bad days, did not manifest themselves. Vivien was the one who had to be kept from dipping ever more frequently into the depravity that came as part and parcel of her illness.

It was in 1953 that he had gone along with Vivien Leigh to star with her and Dana Andrews in *Elephant Walk,* a picture that, like so many others, was cursed from the word go.

Vivien's miraculous beauty had captured Finchy years before in Australia, and now he was certainly her slave. A kind man and patient, he could put up with her terrifying changes of mood, her violence even, and comfort her in her fear. Everybody considered Finchy the perfect companion, nanny, lover for the frequently demented Vivien.

They flew together first to India, then to Hollywood to start the picture. They were warned by the big boys they were to be discreet. Hollywood was still in the hands of the major studios, and actors, no matter how big to the public, had to toe the line. Most of them were under crippling contracts. The new breed like Streisand, Redford, McQueen, Reynolds and Eastwood hadn't yet emerged to shake the studios to their senses.

Elephant Walk started with a dicey script. Finchy was trying to stay ascetic as he did before every picture, eating practically nothing but a lettuce leaf now and then to ensure that hollow look that his audiences interpreted as emotion. Dana Andrews was a well-known swallow and Vivien was clinging vicariously to sanity. A good start. The film was set in India and some location shots were first filmed in Ceylon. Vivien had spent many of her childhood years in India and the climate and nature of Ceylon threw her into a melancholic state that continued to plague her as they continued toward the film city. Such periods of instability brought with them also the symptoms of nymphomania, the indiscriminate lusts that must have been hard on her companions. By the time shooting was to begin for real, she was a near basket case.

Finchy described how utterly impossible she became, drinking heavily straight out of the bottle, tearing her clothes off and running around the streets and their garden naked, throwing dangerous objects at her best friends, or through windows and at passing cars. She had gone over. The studio fired her and sent for Sir Laurence. Filming went on without her as Larry arrived and, sedated, she was brought home to England on a stretcher. Elizabeth

Taylor took her place. Finchy kept his head down and got to work. He and Elizabeth became good friends.

Cast in "Elephant Shit," as the picture came to be known, were a troupe of lady elephants who were supposed, at the climax of the picture, to maraud through the fabricated great mansion that housed the stars and break everything in sight. All props, from cocktail glasses to the piano, had been constructed from material that came apart at the slighest touch.

"All set. Action!" screamed the director. Dead silence.

"Where are the fucking animals?" he bawled.

"Coming," called the elephant trainer.

"Let's take it again. Action!" In trooped the elephants. So dainty were they that they stepped around every obstacle and slid out in file through the French windows. The director was amazed. "They're supposed to break the place apart, for Christ's sake! What is this?"

"Solly, master," whimpered the poor Indian expert. He gave the girls a talking to. It took the poor terrified, too-well-trained elephants five days to give a convincing performance.

Everybody was hysterical. True to Murphy's Law, if anything can go wrong, it will, and a further episode added to the strain. One English actor, well known for his characterizations of foreign gentlemen in the movies, had been cast as the elephant trainer, a baddie. In the script one of the elephants takes her revenge by lifting him in her trunk and squeezing the life out of him. Although mad keen to do the part, he explained that it would be impossible because elephants were his particular nightmare. "They frighten the life out of me."

The studio dragged out the elephant's trunk that had been used in the movie *The Greatest Show on Earth.*

"There you are now. That can't harm you, can it?"

Greatly comforted that his body would be handled by a mechanical trunk with a man on a crank out of sight of the camera, the actor happily threw himself into the part, acting for his life in the scene where the trunk comes into view and picks him up. As his screams became ear-bursting, the other actors and crew thought he just might be overplaying. And besides, he was supposed to be saying his lines in mockup Indian. Then they realized the mechanical trunk had gone freak and no one could stop it. The actor was invalided out of the picture with seven broken ribs. "Just goes to show," they said, shaking their heads.

Finchy returned to England. "Elephant Shit" had been his first major role in Hollywood and he hadn't enjoyed it. Vivien's macabre behavior during the shooting, overflowing into horrendous scenes during their private hours, had quite shaken him, experienced as he was by then with the vagaries of her behavior. Happily for all, that other beautiful actress, Elizabeth Taylor, had been available. Finchy was to know her well in future years, but only through pictures that he never actually made, for example, *Cleopatra,* a number we shall speak of later.

By the time Finchy got home, Vivien was on her feet again and raring to go. Olivier was not so sure he could take much more of the debilitating antics that accompanied her gothic moods, and Finchy, although still besotted with the irresistible "Puss," as she was called, found a greater attraction in the company and comradeship of Olivier himself. Practically one of the family now, along with a very few close and tender friends, Finchy spent many a weekend at Notley Abbey, the Oliviers' country home. The couple's affair was acknowledged and tolerated. Tamara was bought a house in Kensington and when Finchy, who had left the nest, needed a bed, which he seldom did, he slept at Ma's.

His charisma, at least where women were concerned, never failed Finchy. He had some sort of romantic, give-it-to-me-*now* look. He carried that aura of romance and sexuality on his sleeve, making an irresistible impression. Powerful, sexy, romantic—a combination of all of the things a woman is trained to look for in a man. There was a moody, blessed mystery about him and it never failed.

True to his breed of man, he didn't limit himself to his true love but sowed his wild oats among many a willing valley in the heart of London.

To her credit, his agent, Olive Harding, of M.C.A, persuaded her favorite boy away from his messy entanglements to star in a movie in Australia, and he set sail on one of his favorite conveyances, the cargo boat, normally set aside for beat-out captains, penurious menopausal schoolteachers, cripples and eccentrics, usually twelve passengers all told. God *knows* what he found in all that . . . part of his penance to his muse, perhaps. Not even I, who, I believe in my true heart, knew him more than any other human alive, could ever get him to describe his need to be in midocean Atlantic in midwinter in middle madness walking the prow at moonlight. Who am I, though, to question destiny, when destiny was sending that brilliant nutcase across the seas to Australia, and destiny was arranging for a hurricane to blow him and his cargo boat right onto my beach in South Africa. It proves, simply, that history is just not one damn thing after another. Or does it?

6

SITTING ON THE BEACH in Durban, South Africa, I was holding my mother's hand and watching the sailor stroll up and down at the water's edge.

It was 1957 and I didn't want to be there. I wanted to be back in dear old London, where I was on the point of starting my first West End play. The sailor never seemed to tire of his ambling and after an hour I realized there was more to this promenade than had first seemed apparent. He was flirting with me, a very serious, raunchy look in his dark eyes. I turned on my stomach.

Lorrie Jaffe came over and hunched down beside me.

"Good morning, Mrs. Turnbull," he addressed my mother. She nodded vaguely.

"How's things, YoYo?"

"Well, you know," I replied.

"Yes, I know."

Everyone knew that Mother was having one of her little breakdowns and we were here after the shock treatment in Johannesburg for her convalescence. The treatment had worked, but she still had a tendency to hang over the balcony at an unnerving angle and wander off determinedly into the breakers. I was thinking of getting her a dog lead.

"Well, YoYo, my horse won yesterday."

"Great," I said, wondering why they always let you know afterward. "You should have told me."

"Ha-ha, yes. But I will next time. Always remember, Yo, if there's anything I can do?"

I thanked him and he sauntered back to his group of lizards.

I glanced over at the group. The sailor was approaching them. He must be desperate, I thought. Also, he'll find out pretty quick that his kind of South Africans don't like talking to strangers who look the way he did. Barefoot, jeans, no shirt! Oh boy, was that sailor going to find out!

Less than two minutes later, Jaffe was back with the sailor.

"Yo? I've got a nice chap for you to meet. His name is Peter Finch."

Just the day before, I had seen Peter Finch at the local cinema in *A Town Like Alice.* What the hell was he doing ambling along our shores, I asked him, after the usual well-mannered if slightly hysterical greeting.

"You are wonderful!" I gushed.

After thanking me with a rather solemn face, he looked down at Mum.

"Mummy, this is Peter Finch, you know?" Blank. "The actor we saw yesterday in the film about Australia."

She gazed vacantly at Lorrie Jaffe. "Yes, dear." Oh well!

Finchy looked at me. "You have very beautiful legs," he said gravely, and lit up a Woodbine.

He was nearly as black as a black. He sat down in the sand, showing his rather unusual pigeon chest and the very slight hump he had on his back. You could tell he didn't have a stitch on under his faded jeans. The beach seemed entirely focused on him. I could imagine the yackity-yack.

"Why are you here?" I asked. "In Durban, for goodness' sake!"

"It's all very unusual," he replied. "I was on a cargo boat on my way to Australia to make a picture. Last night a hurricane blew up. The ship had to come into Durban harbor for shelter."

"God! That *is* strange!"

"Can you have dinner tonight?" Straight out. No waiting about with this man. I explained that I, mother and father were going to the circus, not, as I had suggested to my father, that the circus was the most tranquil way of entertaining a semidemented mother. "It'll take her mind off it," he had said. "It's all in the mind anyway." Yes, dear father, that's just where it all is. Finchy looked downcast.

"I'm sure you can come, too. Would you like to?"

He smiled. "If I can sit next to you."

A real flirt. But Finchy was handsome and he was somebody, and being impressionable, I was very glad that the family threesome was going to be invaded by a breath of fresh air and someone from my beloved profession.

After a macabre evening at the circus, during which the clown had given mother a bucketful of paper cuttings in the face and she had been made more nervous by the attention of a baby chimpanzee, we returned to our hotel. After helping my father dose up mother and bed her down, Finchy and I took off for the nightclub by the sea.

On this first night, Finchy was wearing a dark suit and a maroon knit tie. He looked very handsome, although when he smiled he had the habit of half covering his mouth. When he once threw back his head and laughed, I saw why. A whole lot of teeth were missing on each side. I wondered if, like Marlene Dietrich, he had had them removed to achieve that hollow look, but when I asked him, he replied something like, "Ah, the vicissitudes of time. I've never been to a dentist in my life."

"Well, you should," I told him.

We talked and drank. He was clever, knew many things and was one of Nature's gentlemen. At one point, two burlies at the bar started shoving each other around. Finchy got to his feet and went over. "No, fellas," he said. "Don't fight, mates, don't fight." Before he left them, the boys had their arms around each other and were singing a stupidly funny ethnic song. Finchy just couldn't stand violence. It brought out the priest in him.

I drove him to his ship and he tried to kiss me. I wasn't playing. "Come to lunch on the boat tomorrow?"

"Yes."

The following day I joined him for lunch with the captain. The ship was leaving at three and I felt honestly sorry that he had to go. I was always lonely in South Africa, feeling like a one-eyed creature in the land of the blind. This man had a lot of gentleness and humor. He'd walked into my life and was walking out.

"I'll write to you from Aussie," he said. "And I want you to call Ma when you get back to London so's I know where to find you. Right?" He kissed me again. "I've fallen in love with your legs."

"What about my head? I've got one, you know."

"Heads come later," he replied.

That was not true with Finchy. For him a woman didn't need a head. Admitting to being a male chauvinist, he said he liked his women to swing from the trees. But this was later, much later in our lives.

I watched the small boat move away over the horizon. Australia was a long way away. I was happy I hadn't given in to the amorous actor: ships that pass in the night. I suppose that's the last time I'll ever see you, I thought.

But within a few hours, I received a cable from the ship: "I miss you. Peter." Until I left for London a couple of weeks later, I received other cables from him. I telephoned his mother and met her and his stepsister, Flavia. I felt a distinct antagonism on the part of Flavia, who, I believe, had fallen in love with Finchy. I was proved right. Ma, on the other hand, was more used to her son's love variations and I don't think she gave the matter particular attention. She had the languid, southern belle sort of personality that nothing seems to disturb—almost, you could say, she was blasé. Peter had written to her about me, she said.

I got my first letter from him. It read:

> My darling, I love you and miss you so much. I want to hold you in my arms and feel you close to me—but I will have to wait—will you? I've started off badly. Just got up to Post Augusta and the bloody conjunctivae (conjunctivitis) decided to get bad and now I'm laid up with a most impressive bandage on one eye—Doc says I can't act till it's alright. Poor old Joe Janni (producer) is pulling his hair out . . . they've

already lost time with weather. Don't be too naughty while I'm away . . . not that I'll know, but I can't bear the thought of it. I love you. I love you. Peter.

So there we were, having a love affair. It frightened me because although I knew that men fall in love with their eyes and a woman with her ears, I couldn't feel that either of us had had the time to reach that point.

Another letter told me:

I dream both waking and sleeping of having you. I explore in my imagination your hips, your thighs. I want to kiss you and love you and watch you and bathe you and make you (three times) and be savage and tender and brutal and be known of you . . . Peter.

Finchy was going very fast indeed. It reminded me of the story told about Tallulah Bankhead at the height of her success on Broadway. After a brilliant first night, she arrived at a party given for her to celebrate the success. As she arrived, a young man pounded across the room to her side. "I'm crazy for you, I adore you, worship you. I'm going out of my mind. I must have you. I want to fuck you." The cool belle replied, "But of course, dahling." "When—when?" beseeched the besotted lover. "Later, dahling, later tonight. I'll see you back at my place at four. And if I'm late, dahling, just start without me."

It seemed to me that Finchy had done just that. The letters kept coming. He accused me of being a lousy correspondent. I was. He wrote:

We can perhaps have a few days in Portugal or Rome when I get back. I do wish you'd start looking for a flat that would suit us . . . must have a nice kitchen and lots of mirrors! Beloved, I dream of you a lot, which is not good enough. I want to feel you in my arms . . . how exciting it is . . . we have so many things to do together.

Reading Finchy's letters now, it seems he had been taken by the "lightning strike." I was flattered. His descriptions of Australia were very beautiful, too. Once he wrote:

> In the bush now . . . we're rather like an army camp and strangely enough one settles down to the same lethargic existence. Terribly healthy and terribly boring. My mate that I spend my whole time with, is Johnny Cadell, the Aborigine who plays Wangal and truly he's the most enchanting person here and the best horseman I have ever seen. He rides like poetry and is my teacher in bushlore. I hope you will be glad to hear there are no women here, except a cook and a continuity girl. . . . I wish you were so that we could walk together in the cool evenings under the stars. . . .

The movie was *Robbery Under Arms,* a story of a heroic bandit taken from Australia's treasure trove of legendary baddies, rougher by far than Robin Hood, but along the same lines. The film also starred David McCallum, who was to become American TVs "Invisible Man"; Jill Ireland, soon to be Mrs. David McCallum and now Mrs. Charles Bronson; and Maureen Swanson, now Lady Dudley. Finchy was back where in the old days he had played the bush cowboy for real:

> Wish you could share the beauty of the salmon rocks, the pale blue gums that stand like ghosts in moonlight. This is the most glorious country, full of time and death and easy life-giving. It puts one in the right philosophic perspective. It dwarfs our small endeavours and makes the truths apparent. I am more and more convinced that you are one of my truths. . . . Believe! Our "piece" moves on slowly. We are about 4 days behind schedule so should be home about April 1. I have saved a lot of lolly, which I can convert into lire . . . so Rome? The bloody eye is improving slowly, but I can't work for another three days at least. I wish you were here to comfort me. I've got a sort of character here with "Moonlight"* that I didn't quite intend. He's come out like some terrible Sicilian bandit . . . as cheeky as hell and a killer at the same time. Oh! My God, how I want you. I lie and dream of having you and pray that you want me as much as I want you. My kisses—all of them are for you. My love, my love, Peter.

Funny, he was never Finchy to himself. Nor was he Finchy to me. I don't remember that we ever called each other by our given

* *Captain Moonlight,* a film title.

names. To each other we weren't Peter and Yolanda. We were nameless lovers . . . dearlings.

A kangaroo shoot was organized on location. He was horrified.

> Tonight we went for a Kangaroo shoot. I am doubly a Buddhist. Oh my God, they shot three poor bleeding living things. Do you mind if I become more and more of a Buddhist? When I take you to the Ox on the Roof in London . . . it's veggies for me! By the way, I have written sixteen letters to you and not had one back. I love you so and will talk to Tamara and get a divorce as soon as possible . . . then you can live with me or marry me if and what you will. Don't be frightened. I love you and think I can make you happy . . . as happy as I can. Do you love me? Peter.

Roseland, the play I hoped would establish me as at least a promising newcomer, opened and closed within six nights. I was desolate, although critically I had been praised. The whole cast suffered the shock of being given the bird by the gallery. I, a mere beginner, was so angry at them, I felt like stepping forward at the single curtain call and telling them to go and get knotted. Instead, I stood along with the others and took it, like the pros we were. One of the cast shot himself after the play closed. The writer and director, Anthony Pelissier, never tried a play again. It was a number one bomberoo and everyone in our business gets one and that's probably all one can take. In later days the cliques of gallery hooters were silenced, but at that time, the profession was terrified of them.

Finchy arrived back. I didn't want him to move in and take me over. He had left Tamara years before and slept mostly at Ma's or wherever he felt like settling. His affair with Vivien had come to the crunch when Sir Laurence had faced Finchy with the dreaded ultimatum: "If you want her, you'd better take her." Finchy rapidly started to break the hold. Scarlett O'Hara was not supposed to end up that way. Wasn't in the script. I was so dumb I didn't even know about the affair and Finchy was very discreet. Obsessed with my future in the theater, I was damn sure that if I let Finchy move into my bed-sitting-room at Dolphin Square, he would take my mind off things I knew were in the long run much more important than love. I wanted to be a star.

I held out for nearly six months. Finchy slept outside on the doormat. One day I fell in love with him and he moved in. I wondered why I had bothered to make him wait. For him it had a certain piquancy—and of course he had won in the end.

7

FINCHY WAS a tremendously popular man. He was amiable, full of laughter; his endless anecdotes, however oft repeated, delighted his friends. Other actors liked him and to the units and crews at the film studios he was "good old Finchy." He always drank a fair amount, but he was very much the happy drunk and generous to a fault. He was well known in London for inviting the "whole flaming place for a drink on me, mates." The "whole flaming place" could sometimes consist of a hundred people. "It's only lolly, luv."

One of his favorite haunts was the Casa Pepe, a rundown pseudo Spanish restaurant in the Fulham Road run by East-Enders. The entertainment was provided, apart from Finchy, by a somber cockney boy pretending to be from Toledo and a couple of girls from Eastbourne masquerading as flamenco dancers. There was a lot of noise and simulated passion, with whirling skirts and glowering expressions, and Finchy, surrounded by his entourage, which included the odd stray Aussie mate who'd looked him up and a straggle of about six chicks of varied ages, reputation, previous entanglements and beauty, depending on how you looked at it. His stepsister invited other "old friends" so that the females far outnumbered the males, which suited our man just fine. Finchy was in his element when he could lie back at the head of a table and throw his benign smile at a surrounding bevy of women. He loved women . . . the harem bugged me wild. I knew most of these girls had been there once and a couple of them indicated they wouldn't mind being back. On the whole, they ignored me.

One night when Finchy was encouraging a hopeless though pretty black girl to sing, a well-known failed Rank starlet remarked, "Your crown's slipping, ducky!"

I didn't reply, just smiled back trying to look bitchy as hell and come up with some devastating crack to wipe the grin off her face. I was paralyzed with jealousy and sulked the rest of the evening. I'm happy to say that particular adversary ended up in a bar in the Balearics.

Finchy was known as a great lover and with his career going at leaps and bounds, I could understand why he was a honeypot for women. It seemed to me that he'd had every woman in London, including the "ladies" of the night, who never failed to give him a wave from the pavements around Mayfair as we sailed by in a taxi. "'Allo, Finchy! 'Ow you doing, then?" He'd thrust his head out of the window and call, jerking a thumb in my direction, "Got her now, see?"

I felt quite proud until one night he went decidedly too far. We spent a lot of evenings at the White Elephant, a showbiz restaurant in Curzon Street along the lines of Broadway's Sardi's, where everybody goes to see and be seen and eat the chopped liver. After a gay evening, Finchy suggested we walk a little before getting a taxi home. It was a clear spring London night and the "girls" stood out prettily in front of the buildings and at corners. This was before someone cleaned up the streets and made them all go away, downstairs somewhere. We walked toward Hyde Park Corner with Finchy answering an occasional wave and cheeky greeting. "Where you been then, with your big black prick?" inquired one. Finchy chortled happily. "Nice kids," he said. I bet, I thought. I knew very well now that Finchy had a thing in his mind about having two women together. Esthetically, he had explained, there's nothing like it. "No man can satisfy two women," I snorted huffily.

"I'd like to have another girl make love to you, darling. It would be so beautiful."

I primly explained that I didn't fancy the idea of another girl making love to me. "I'm not queer, you see," remembering the days at school. To play and touch and do with another girl things meant for a man and a woman—well frankly, no.

A small white sports car cruised up beside us. There were two girls in the front, one a blonde, the other a redhead. The car pulled up and the blonde leaned out of the window. Oh, Jesus, I thought, here we go and I hope not, because I really can't face this. It's not me. Please God, don't let him go through with it.

"Finchy bags! 'Aven't seen you for ages, luv. What's the matter, luv? Can't do it anymore?" Ha-ha. Finchy glanced at me. I couldn't tell how inebriated he was or if he might just be feeling a little *mêchant*. He did have that crooked smile and was twinkling . . . that's when he would get up on his toes and sort of hop. He turned the collar of his suit up and that, like "fighting" with his hat, was a bad sign. It meant he wanted to go off to the "wild wet woods," and right now the "woods" had something to do with these ladies. He pulled me toward the car.

"This is my mate, Yolande."

"Hello." Nervous smile.

"Hello, luv, so it's you whose bin keeping the old cock busy, eh?" Charming.

"Well, er, we're engaged, you see."

The blonde smiled. "Well, come on, then, git in. We must celebrate."

The redhead leaned across. "Yeah, come up to our place for a drinkie. Come on, then." I was hanging back.

"Well, um, Finchy's got to work tomorrow." Screams of laughter.

"You don't know him very well, do you, ducky? He acts better when he's bin at it all night. Isn't that so, luv?"

"Okay," said Finchy, "we'll come along for one."

"No, we won't," I said.

"Aw, don't be silly, come on. We're just going to have a drinkie, aren't we, Finchy?"

"Come along, Yo. You'll be safe with me, and these are my mates."

He pushed me into the back of the car. I mustn't get into this, I kept thinking. Why does he want to test me this way? Isn't he happy with me? Don't I give him enough love? The car was heading for Covent Garden.

"My name's Sharon," said the blonde, "and she's Marianne."

I stared at the back of their heads. Got to get out, got to get out. I whispered to Finchy to let me out.

He giggled. "Look, baby, you got to learn to relax. You're like a boat that's always tied to the quay. Let it go."

I began to think. Maybe I was a little bourgeoise. After all, I was old enough to go up to a whore's pad and see some of the action that my dearly beloved had partaken of for years. If I was going to marry him, I had better find out all about his little cravings. No? Well, no, I answered myself. Not really. But I went on sitting there. Just what kind of scene could I make at this point. I'd better sit tight and pretend.

We parked outside a tall building that looked like a warehouse. It was very dark. One of the girls used two keys to open the big door. It was pitch black until she turned on a single unshaded bulb that hung in the passage. Peter took hold of my hand and we followed the girls up the narrow staircase, lighting the second bulb on the landing just as the first one went out. On the second floor we arrived at a brown glazed door. Sinister. Sharon rang the bell and whacked the door with her fist three times. Eventually an ancient crone appeared.

"'Allo, auntie. All right luv?" Without a word the woman swayed drunkenly back down the corridor and disappeared.

"Poor old fart," said Sharon.

"Well, you got to have someone in this trade," remarked the other.

I wondered what protection the "old fart" could be if it came to the crunch. We followed the girls into a large bed-sitting-room overlooking the street. Everything here seemed to be red. Red light bulbs, carpet, candlewick bedspreads, sofa. It looked like hell. Very tidy, though.

"Got a lovely new bottle of scotch here. Look, Finchy." The girl lifted a bottle of whiskey from a small table. The glasses were set out and a jug of water. She held out the bottle to me. I nodded. I'm going to need that stuff, I thought, as I perched nervously on one of the bunks. The blonde handed round the drinks and started to undress. She got down to her red garter belt, frilled heart-shaped bikini that I knew she had bought at Weiss in Piccadilly, because I had a pair of the same, and black stockings. Marianne followed suit.

"Come on, darling, show them your lovely self."

I started to peel slowly, still sitting, and shoved my dress behind me. The girls took me in. I was also wearing stockings and garters. We all did in those days. It was before women's lib and the psychological protection of panty hose was not yet available. It was the mad fifties and women were just beginning to realize that sex was easy to have without getting pregnant or feeling guilty about it. Orgasms were in!

"What are you waiting for, mate?" Sharon asked Finchy. "'Asn't dropped off, 'as it?"

I crossed my legs and Marianne sat down beside me.

"Off with the panties, girls. Ooh, Finchy, I thought you liked to fight for it!"

Finchy was beginning to look uncomfortable. I was doing my best with a false smile and bright eyes. He started to take off his suit. He got down to his shirt and socks, then settled on the sofa with his scotch. He was staring at me. You stupid bastard, I thought, how are we going to get out of this? I turned to Marianne.

"What's a nice girl like you—"

"Doing in a job like this?" she finished for me. "Well, luv, it's like this, y'see. I've got a little kid in Ireland. I love that little bastard—and he is. I want to work and make enough money for him to 'av a sort of life, you know? He's three."

"God, I think that's wonderful." I was full of admiration for her.

"It's not a bed of roses, my dear, I can tell you. We get some right fuckers in 'ere. I've got one wants me to be a bloody poodle. He puts a lead round me neck and I have to bark so he comes, the asshole."

"Isn't it dangerous?"

"Christ, most of them are stark ravers. That's why Sharon and I work together. Oh, boy, you couldn't do this job alone, I can tell you."

Sharon had herself at Finchy's knees, her mouth trying to tackle his strangely reluctant tool. I decided to rise above the whole thing. I started to chat to my friend Marianne. She was a really nice girl, with long, thick hair, white, freckled skin and lovely big tits. I'd always wanted big boobs, so I admired them.

"No, luv, you're much better off with your little ones. They'll never droop, dear. See me in twenty years. I'll be able to sweep the carpet with them."

"For Christ's sake, this isn't a bloody tea party," exploded Finchy. "Go down on her."

"Go down on her yourself," I riposted. "It was your bloody idea!"

"Eh, Finchy, your bleedin' cock's dead, mate."

"Oh shit," sighed Finchy. "I knew it. I'd never be able to do it with her."

I got up. I was nearly in tears. "It's not my fault. It's just not my scene. You shouldn't have brought me. Have your 'wild wetters,' but leave me out of them, you silly bugger."

By now he was about as rampant as a lesbian at an Elk convention.

"Aw, come on, Marianne, let's try and get the old boy up," said Sharon. "Come and give us a bit."

She lay down along the floor, and Marianne obediently went down between her legs. I watched and Finchy watched me. Sod you, you tit, I thought, you made me join the square dance and I am not going to run. He sat there with his dispossessed angel of love between his legs. Sharon glanced over Marianne's head at him.

"For Christ's sake, Finchy, what happened to your lovely black prick, then?" She glanced at me. "It's no good, luv," she said to Marianne. "I think the old bugger is in love with her. When they're in love they can never make it with another woman." I was beginning to feel better. Maybe we could go home now.

"Bloody waste of time," said Finchy, getting up. "I'm off."

"That'll be fifty quid, matey."

"What for? We haven't done anything." He was getting dressed fast.

"I don't care if we haven't done anything, mate. It's the time, see. Time is money."

Finchy was making for the door. "Balls," he said.

"Well, I'm not so sure about that, kiddo. Just let's have what you owe."

Marianne and I were getting dressed.

"Come on, darling, you've got to pay," I said.

"I haven't got any money!"

"Don't try kidding us, mate," from a chorus of three.

"Finchy, you bloody pay."

"No!" and he made a run for it. We heard him thundering down the stairs, laughing.

"Right, you bastard," said Sharon, "we'll have you."

"You're damn right we will," we agreed in unison. The three of us took off after the escaping giggler. As we hit the street, we saw him take a cab.

"He'll be going back to our place," I said.

"Right." The three of us piled into the white sports car.

"Where to, luv?"

"Beauchamp Place."

"He was there, all right, hiding under the blankets in bed. I was very firm with him.

"You are going to pay, my love, if I have to ring Olive Harding."

Ollie, as I've said, was Finchy's agent and he was petrified of her.

"No," he cried. "No. Anything but Auntie Ollie."

"Well pay, you bugger."

Now the naughty boy. "Haven't got a checkbook."

"Money?"

"No money." He hunched under the bedclothes.

I got my checkbook. "Okay, you make it out here and change the name of the bank to yours. Honestly, Finchy, you are the end."

We stood over him while he made out the check and sulkily handed it over. "You're a bunch of bloody Valkyries," he said. "Man's not safe these days."

What cheek, I thought. I said, "They may be whores, but they deserve every penny they made. Especially if they have to deal with schleppers like you!" And I gave Finchy an echoing slap on his upturned behind.

With his usual amnesia, Finchy, when he woke in the morning, had completely forgotten the incident and it was never mentioned again. The experience, however, did not dampen his obsession to have me, sooner or later, with another of the fair sex. I knew last night wasn't going to be the last time. And it wasn't. But the next time I left him.

8

IT WAS AMUSING that we were still living in my bed-sit cum bath and kitchen on Beauchamp Place in Knightsbridge and I was paying the rent. I was supposed to be the "heiress" from South Africa and darling Finchy never had a penny. Auntie Ollie took care of all that. We ate out and signed for it, we drank out and signed for it. The only thing we didn't do out was make love. We made love in and I paid for it.

We were in love with each other, and true to form, I was jealous if he stood too close to anyone, even a man, and he was outraged at the very idea of being cuckolded. His outlook, caused, I suppose, by lack of self-esteem, drove me up the wall. Never one to fancy waiters or sailors, however sweet, I was forever accused of giving them the come-on. Aboard ship, a pleasant glance at a man's face when ordering a drink or a sick bag meant to Finchy that I harbored a terrible lust to possess the innocent attendant. Finchy should have known that it is power that attracts me rather than servility. The former relaxes me, while the latter reminds me how unjust the world is. But how were we going to discuss that one? I tried to discuss many things with Finchy, but he had hidden away many, many things and they were never spoken of.

After the fracas in Covent Garden with the ladies of the night I innocently prayed that my dedicated body would be enough for him. I did try to probe his mind for thoughts on the subject of threesomes, but gave up in the face of his loss of memory in all things disturbing to him. Amnesia is a gift. As for Vivien, she seemed to have disappeared from his life entirely. He never spoke of her and because I was the new girl in London, nobody even told me there had been a great affair.

It did strike me that Ma and Flavia behaved toward me as if I were a here-today gone-tomorrow bird whom Finchy was making the most of. They knew, of course, that the Olivier marriage was in a death struggle to survive and that Olivier had found a young, superlative actress named Joan Plowright and that secretly Vivien had been in touch with Ma, who was trying to bring about a reunion between her son and the shattered Viv. The collapse of the marriage of the theatrical Royal Family, the Oliviers, had sent Leigh into intolerable rages that broke up rehearsals at the Royal Court Theatre, where Larry was directing Plowright. Vivien's insulting behavior with friends and enemies alike finally brought her into the hands of doctors who, by this time, had more effective techniques for dealing with her illness. But she had lost Larry. It was amazing that Finchy, the very essence of chaos, had declined when Olivier had offered him Viv. Ma was still trying, however, and later I was to learn that Vivien, a compulsive letter writer, had been sending love notes to Finchy for months. Letters he never answered.

Finchy had a very real fear that all women were unfaithful and that it was only a matter of time before I would find someone younger or richer or with a bigger cock. It wore me down trying to reassure him and make him feel safe and loved. Furthermore, it's very insulting to be falsely accused. He was man enough for me and for many years the only man.

One day he arrived back at Beauchamp Place to find me on the phone with an old admirer who hadn't given up. Finchy went white and accused me of being unfaithful.

"What do you mean, unfaithful?"

"You're talking to a lover."

"Don't be ridiculous! It's Desmond Lewis."

"I don't give a fuck who it is."

"Oh, don't be so bloody silly. How can I be faithless on the telephone. Ah, excuse me, Desmond—can I call you back? . . . Finchy, I was only *talking* to the man!"

He turned on his heel. "I'm leaving."

I saw that he was sober. "Finchy!"

"It's too much," he said, and walked out. What a tit, I thought, and let him go.

A few days later, missing him, I called Ma. "Where is he?" I asked gingerly, knowing she'd enjoy telling me he must have gone off to the "wild wet woods."

"Oh, didn't you know, dear? He's gone to Africa to make *The Nun's Story.*"

The Nun's Story, with Audrey Hepburn, was directed by Fred Zinnemann, one of the great directors, and it was a break into international films for Finchy, but he certainly left egg all over my face through the spite of his fevered imagination. Typical.

Twelve weeks later, as I hung out my window like Carmen in heat, I saw the bronzed him come around the corner. He was looking up and I called down to him that I loved him and that he was a ruthless bastard. When he came upstairs and into my arms, he explained: "I retreated in the face of the enemy, Yo."

I didn't stay angry for long. One never did with that man. At least he had proved to me in his own way that he didn't want and wouldn't take any competition for his woman. He wanted me beside him and not even my career was going to interfere with that.

He had a wanderlust and it was deep. I was also a natural vagabond, in that I loved just going away, anywhere and anytime. We left London whenever we could, leaving piles of scripts for Auntie Ollie to read—Finchy never bothered with them. Although a true journeyman actor, the sort of actor—and one of the few of his day and age—who, if being a mummer consisted in playing night stands at next to nothing a week, would, as long as the piece was quality, still be an actor. And the desire wasn't for fame or fortune; he really only wished to be respected by his peers. But traveling was his alternative life and we embarked on it across the world. It wasn't that easy traveling with him, for the simple reason that he had an insane urge to get lost, lose his passport, forget his coat, miss the train (although never the boat), get blind drunk on airplanes . . . and he never, never booked a hotel at the other end, the other end usually being some unheard-of island off a lost continent. It wasn't always fun, but when you love, you pay the toll for your beloved's ways.

Returning a couple of months later from Ibiza, one of the Balearic islands which in the late fifties was untouched by the tourist trade and was where Finchy had made one of his amazing magic acquisitions—he had purchased a farm from a man who didn't own it (an often-repeated—I think subconscious—formula to make it unnecessary to have roots), we settled back into Beauchamp Place. I was beginning to wonder if we'd ever get out of there.

Marriage, as a subject, was cropping up. I dreaded the idea, having lived through my mother and father's. I thought marriage was a love killer and Finchy had been heard to say that "the little piece of paper" was a blight on romance. Honestly, I didn't give a damn, although my womb was sending messages to my head about having a lovely baby that looked like us. I thought I'd have one anyway. Like many young women, my plan was to have a baby with every man I loved, making a children's paradise populated by me, as Mother Earth, the babies, and all the beautiful male subjects I'd chosen to propagate with. When one's young, what do you know? Finchy was to be my first perfect offspring's papa. Flooded with spermatozoa though I was, however, there were no signs of new life. Hopes of being one of the earth's best baby kilns were dashed, Naturally I blamed him. He'd used up all his good stuff. For fun, we kept trying. I don't think he knew what I had in mind, but my enthusiasm for him sexually was colored by a happy new dimension.

One afternoon, Ma called. Finchy spoke to her. "Ma wants us to go over to the house."

"Why?"

"She just wants us to go over."

"I don't like it there. You always get pissed and all your old drinking mates and dancing girls get asked over."

"Come on. We must."

We got into a taxi. I was cross.

"Why must we?"

"Because Vivien's there."

"What?"

"Vivien wants to see me. She's been writing to me."

Vivien Leigh—Scarlett O'Hara wanted to see Finchy?

"What does she want to see you about?" My womb was opening and closing like a fist.

"Ma says she wants me back."

I gasped. Scarlett O'Hara wanted my lover back. I was appalled. "And are you—are you? . . . Why doesn't she ask Clark Gable—Rhett back?" My darling Finchy! He'd never be able to say no. "Oh, poor Scarlett—Vivien—oh, how awful—terrible."

"Now, stop that." Finchy seemed very calm. He'd decided. I sat back, feeling wounded and wobbly and tragic. I hoped I wasn't pregnant from this morning.

The cabbie pulled up outside Ma's door.

"I'm not coming in," I said. "I couldn't face it. Losing you."

"You're not going to lose me. I love you." He took my hand and pulled me gently onto the street. Then why did he need me there, I wondered.

"I love you, too," I said.

Ma opened the door of the small mews house. Some comedown from Tara as a backdrop for Scarlett.

"Vivien is here, darling," she greeted Finchy with her toothless Southern belle smile. I'm never really going to like you, Ma, I decided. Never really did and never really will. You are trying to fuck up our love.

"Come in, dears."

She was half lounging on the sofa facing us, her dainty feet up on the cushions. She was wearing a softly pastelled silk dress, and her legs were pretty. She smiled that lethal pussycat smile at Finchy. I was mesmerized.

"Hello, darling." Her emerald eyes swallowed him and then slid over to me. At me.

"Hello, Puss." He walked over and bent to kiss her.

"This is Yolande, Puss." I almost curtsied. She was terribly grand, even reclined. I'd been in love with Scarlett since I'd bribed my way into a fleabag cinema in Johannesburg at the age of twelve. It was banned for the under-eighteens in South Africa, for sex or revolution, I wouldn't know. Out there, they ban books by the Brontës.

"How are you, darling?" she asked him.

For the rest of the interview, she never glanced at me. I subsided into an armchair, and Ma watched and listened with undisguised glee. She was glued. I died.

Vivien leaned forward.

"Darling. Finchy. I want you back." Finchy was perched on an armchair close by her. I wondered how long he'd known there would be this confrontation. Days or weeks. Why was I there?

Vivien went on. "I want to live with you, darling. I love you."

Finchy smiled. "Come on, Puss."

"I need you, darling. I want you."

Finchy got up and went over to Ma. "Get us a drink, luv." Ma scuttled off to attend to the request.

"Darling"—the emerald eyes were imploring—"I'd live in an attic with you. I'd live in a garret with you."

Ma had returned, and Finchy moved across to get his drink. Vivien followed him with her eyes. I nervously studied her. She was still exquisite. The most feminine woman I had ever seen. There was a danger in her face and a sort of gentle mad control showed about her pointed mouth. Her eyes were slightly bloodshot, as if she had been crying. Her body was very still, but her glove-encased hands moved about each other like loving snakes. She opened her alligator handbag and took out a cigarette. Finchy stepped forward to light it and she held his wrist. "Darling?" she whispered.

I felt incredibly uncomfortable and longed to go away from this room where so much was not being said. It was for them, old lovers, to work through. By now I disliked Finchy as well as Ma. What kind of kinks were they? And I felt terribly sorry for Vivien. She looked as if she needed protection. She looked frightened and very fragile. There was something terribly wrong. Finchy was taking his time. Perhaps he was thinking of something Vivien had once said to him a long time ago, but which still galled him. You may be a great actor one day, Peter, maybe. But you'll never be as great an actor as Larry. Yes, perhaps that was it. He was going to take his revenge. That was a part of him I never suspected. Perhaps Vivien had never considered that either. We waited.

"It's too late, Viv. Sorry, luv." There was a short, tight silence. She moved slightly. He looked down at her.

"You see—I'm in love with her." He didn't even bend his head toward my catatonic figure.

"I see," she said. She took us both in, sadly, a little beseechingly. I was heartbroken. Slowly she got to her feet.

"I'll take you to your car, Puss," he said. "You still have the Rolls?"

Vivien Leigh nodded and let him lead her outside. He was back in less than a minute. I'd gotten to my feet, very nervous of the glowering Ma. He took me in his arms.

"I do love you, y'know."

"I'm so glad," I told him, but I was thinking that it had been a cruel way to break a love affair.

"Gosh," I asked him as I clung on, "didn't it hurt?"

"No, not really."

He reminded me of the camel castrator in Tangiers who, in giving a demonstration to a crowd of tourists, separates the legs of the beast, then takes a brick in each hand and goes *thwack,* squeezing the animal's testicles to a pulp.

"Gosh, doesn't that hurt?" inquires one gentleman.

"Not if you keep your thumbs back," explains the castrator.

Finchy could be as hard.

9

NOW THAT FINCHY was separated from Tamara, we had become "officially" engaged. There had been a lot of publicity and speculation about the romance. Was the hell raiser going to tie the knot? Peter told the press that we were going to be married and both be big stars.

Neglecting my own affairs as usual, I went with Finchy up to Scotland, where he was going to play in Robert Louis Stevenson's *Kidnapped*. We stayed at a great old house by the side of a loch. The grounds were enormous and gloriously wild and the black-and-white-faced highland sheep grazed where they would. Exploring, we saw an old chapel and wandered inside, where we found an elderly Scots priest. Both being Scots, me Turnbull and he Campbell or Ingle-Finch, it seemed fated that our liaison should be sanctified there.

Finchy greeted the priest. "Hello, Father, we're staying up at the big house. I'm an actor, Peter Finch, and I'd like to marry Yo here."

"Of course, I'll marry you. It would be a pleasure. You'll have to get a special license if you're in a bit of a rush, but there shouldn't be any problem."

To both of us it seemed perfect there. Simply to marry, just the two of us, almost secretly. We would wear whatever suitable clothes we had and find some old character to be witness. This, we thought, is the way marriages should be made.

We ran back to the house and Finchy put through a call to Auntie Ollie.

"We're getting married on Wednesday," Finchy told her.

"No, you're not, dear," she replied briskly. "You're still married."

"Well, bloody get me unmarried then."

"All I'm saying, dear boy, is that if you get married on Wednesday, which I think is a lovely idea, you'll land in prison. You are still married, dear, and two wives are not allowed in Scotland or England."

"Well, get a divorce. How do you get a divorce?"

"I don't know, dear. I've never tried to get married. I'll find out."

"I don't want to mess about, Ollie. I want to get married this week."

"Well yes, dear, we'll do our best. I'll let you know. Ta-ta."

It never happened. The divorce took longer than either of us could believe. "Bleedin' lawyers. Always want their piece of flesh."

When *Kidnapped* was completed we went back to London. I persuaded Finchey to buy a tiny house in Sydney Street, a steal at £5,000 and just around the corner from the Chelsea Registry Office. Couldn't be more convenient. I started to fix it up. The fact that the previous owner had slit her throat in the kitchen bothered us not at all, although I sometimes heard the swishing of skirts on the stairway and one of our guests saw the head of a white horse sticking through the kitchen/dining server one night. We were as happy as bugs in a rug and I was still trying for a baby.

Finchy started rehearsing for a play called *Two for the Seesaw,* an American comedy written by Bill Gibson, who had had an enormous success with *The Miracle Worker,* a play based on the life of Helen Keller. Arthur Penn, the brilliant future director of *Bonnie and Clyde,* would direct the two-character piece with Finchy and an American actress named Gerry. Rehearsals started at the Haymarket Theatre, a dream of a theater and London's most beautiful.

It was a hard play, and comedy was difficult for Finchy. Also, the American accent is hardly ever played with great success by any European artist. Gerry was an actress from the "realistic" school, very serious, very method.

"It's like peeling an onion, honey," she would husk at Finchy. "Honey, you just gotta go on peeling and peeling until you get there."

"Get where?" inquired Finchy.

"There, man"—she'd strike her chest—"where it's at, y'know, where you feel it."

Oh, boy! Finchy battled on under the faultless Arthur Penn, trying not to be too distracted by the "new way" to act. Gerry had one little piece of business that used to throw him every night. The telephone would ring on the set and she would call out: "Tellllle-phoooooooooone!" She would drag out the word for what seemed at least a minute. It sent Finchy ape.

"Gerry, why can't you just say, 'Telephone'? I mean, it's only the bleedin' telephone, isn't it?"

"No, honey, you just don't understand that's the way she feeeeeeels about the telllllephoooooooooone." Holy Jesus.

The play was a critical success and both actors got good reviews. Gerry was a crazy but sweet crazy girl and I think she was popping coke or something, because she was way out of sight most of the time. A year later, she died in Los Angeles onstage, one of the best ways, they say, for an actor to go.

I was still hovering at the edge of things. Although I was getting offers, it was difficult to accept something that might take me on tour for two months or more. I was beginning to get the reputation of the actress who didn't want to work. It was hard and I knew I was doing myself harm, but love plays havoc with good sense. Finchy kept saying to the press that I was a fine actress and how proud he was of me. "I have no doubts she will make it to the top."

Well, I was doing everything to sabotage myself, because when he wanted me there, I was. I blew the professional chances, and the offers started to come more slowly. I left my own agent, Laurence Evans, also at M.C.A., and joined Olive Harding's stable. From that moment on, I'd had it. Finchy must have given her the red light. Memo to Ollie: *Keep Yo home.*

Another time I wanted to have plastic surgery on my nose.

"I want a little nose that tilts up, like that."

Finchy was appalled. "I'll give you a little nose that tilts—with this." He held out his fist. "The nose stays."

Our relationship was still in the "eternal honeymoon" stage. We were loving and tender with each other. I adored him and he showed a genuine love for me. Now and then I tried to break the possessive hold he had on me. Having met Charlie Feldman, one of the great Hollywood agents, the man who had discovered the most beautiful stars at the beginning, he asked me to dine. I decided I should. I told Finchy, who sulked all afternoon in bed. When evening came and I started to prepare myself to be beautiful, he became very seductive and held me up. The doorbell rang. God, it was Feldman, and I looked as though I'd been pulled through a bush backward. It rang again. Hastily, I threw on a negligee, closed the door on a grinning Finchy and answered the door. Feldman took one look at me and leaped.

"Baby, you look just the way Rita looked the first night I ever saw her!"

"Please," I protested, "I'm not ready."

"You look really ready to me, baby. Where's the bedroom? Um."

The bedroom door opened and there stood old snake hips, naked as the day he was born.

"Evening, mate."

"Oh Christ, it's Finch."

Finchy leaned against the door, all rangy. "Drinkie, Charlie?"

Charles got cool. "Okay, Finch, you've had your laugh. Now I am taking Yolande to dinner. Okay?"

I dressed as quickly as I could and left with Feldman.

"You're killing your chances with that wino."

"But I love him."

"Forget it."

I didn't get my big break from Charles, or Sam Spiegel, or Carl Foreman or a hundred other men who had been eager to give me the chance.

The spreading of the word that Finchy was my permanent lover, in some ways saved me from "the casting couch." Not that Finchy frightened anyone, but he had ways of letting people know when he wasn't happy. He was a big enough star then for people not to want to provoke him, so it became "Hands off YoYo!"

There were some aspects of living with Finchy which could be described as "difficult." His drinking, which was regular and indiscriminate. He had no liver. He could drink champagne and when that ran out, turn to whiskey, gin, brandy or Australian sweet sparkling Sherry. Unless he was on one of his regimens before shooting a picture, he drank every day, starting at noon and carrying on through the day and into the early hours of the morning. He was not an insulting drunk, rather the opposite. He became very sweet when inebriated.

If he was unhappy, though, the signs would begin to show. He would huddle in his chair; his bottom lip, by now ringed with dry red wine, would pout; he would turn up his collar and start waving his fingertips in the air. With this pantomime—it was always played out in silence—he was communicating the mysterious and mischievous approach of his need to be off to the "wild wet woods." This "place" comes from a piece by Kipling, "The Cat That Walked by Himself:" "He went back through the Wild Wet Woods, waving his wild tail, and walking by his wild lone. But he never told anybody." That is what Finchy did, but when had he associated himself with that cat that walked by himself? It must have been a long, long time ago. And the poem came true. He never told anybody about the origins of his need.

No matter how you love a man, living with one who is a real

drinker is debilitating. I became a nurse sometimes, carrying him out of bars and clubs, apologizing to restaurateurs and waiters. And never understanding the reason why he needed to eliminate himself so totally, to become so blind that there was no memory of any of it.

I tried to get him to talk about it, to try to understand it himself, but it was past words and meaning. "I'm never late on the set, mate. They can never say that." At one point, a great fellow drinker, Peter O'Toole, went for a cure. I tried to get Finchy to go.

"I don't even take an aspirin, Yo, you know that. I don't want these fellas messing around with me."

Finchy also suffered under the embarrassing delusion that blacks hung from the trees. When in his mind I started to get a little above my station, he would snap that a woman shouldn't think and what he wanted was "one that hung from the trees." When I asked, "Like who?" he answered me with "A peasant, a geisha, a black girl. They never give you any lip." As a white nigger, that disgusted me.

"You chauvinist."

"That's right. And that's why I like hookers and black girls."

"You don't know a thing about black people, Finchy. I'm more black than you'll ever be. You're a patronizing pig."

I was a South African white girl, a privileged South African white girl, a fact that contained within it a racial dilemma well documented in the annals of psychiatry. From the day I was born, I was brought up by my black family. Rich parents who live in areas where the majority of indigenous people are non-European, like India, South America, the southern states of the United States, even China in the old days, hand their babies over to mammies or amahs and very rarely have contact with them except on the most superficial level: "Did she eat her carrots all down, Betty?" In Africa the wealthy parents are called the White Giants. My years had been spent, from cradle to adolescence, with my black mother, the black cookie, the other servants of the family and their friends, who raised other white babies from other affluent homes. Our mothers were busy at bridge and tennis and parties, and our fathers were making fortunes and traveling abroad.

During these vital, formative years, we loved and were loved and cared for by our Bettys. We absorbed their traditions and thoughts, their love of rhythm, their special music . . . their folk stories, their tribal taboos, their humor, their sexual behavior and last, but by no means least, their fear and hatred of the White Giant.

Flipping back into my memory, I recall a maid and Freddy, the cook, emerging from his bedroom, their glowing faces and their laughter telling me, even at that age, that sex was good and fun and natural. Later, when at pubescence I was dragged squawking from their arms to become part of the foreign tribe of whites, on the assumption that I was now a sexual object and might be horribly violated by my black brother or sister, the break was unspeakably painful. I never understood why we were separated, of course, but the separation psyched me. I was frightened of my parents and their friends; they were so different, and I never understood them, especially their sex. What did they do behind those locked bedroom doors? And why did they never smile when they came out? With the possible exception of my father, the whites treated my black relations like slaves and turds. Niggers.

Being sensitive and perceiving the appalling injustice in that country, I made so many scenes that my parents allowed me to go to London, to finishing school. It was brilliantly entitled to its epithet, the Monkey Club. There I mixed with equally fucked-up white girls from all over the world. South Africa has problems.

As for Finchy and blacks, I went with him a few times to their clubs in the cellars of London, to see if he really had a mystical relationship with them. He didn't. He was patronizing as hell, an unforgivable insult, although the blacks had the humor and understanding to tolerate it. He was only doing his best, but *he* just didn't understand. As soon as he saw a black man or woman, he would go into such a performance, clasping them in his arms like a long-lost relative and calling them mate. It embarrassed the hell out of them at first. They'd look mystified at his indiscriminate love; then, not to hurt his feelings, which were genuine, if misplaced, they'd pat him on the back and walk off, shaking their head. "These crazy white bastards, man!"

They knew him as an actor and a guy who went gaga when pissed, but they didn't treat him like a colleague or a part of their struggle, more like a sentimental, well-meaning actor chappie who hadn't got the story quite straight.

"Just 'cause we're black, Finchy, doesn't make us different from you, old man. There's good and bad among all of us, even you whites. Always some good and always some bad, man."

"Well," Finchy would slur, "me greatest mate is Johnny Cadell and he's an aboriginal."

"What? One of them fuzzy bastards with fuzzy hair, that eats lizards, man?"

"He's me mate. And he's black. Just like you."

"Sheeeeeeeit! You sure got it all wrong, man. We don't like them abbo creeps. They're savages!"

Finchy was no social butterfly. He loathed the powerful and mighty. He disliked high society, and anyone who'd been to an English public school was immediately dubbed a "chinless wonder," whether or not his facial characteristics jibed with the criticism. It goes without saying that what came to be called "jet set" was poison. He accused me of being a snob, because I had friends who were achievers and enjoyed the pleasant things of life, including conversation. Finchy did not have conversations. He either listened to the one or two academics he knew or lectured one on Caesar or Hadrian or poets and poetry or told jokes. I don't think I ever had a discussion with him. I was, after all, just a woman and he was full of self-found knowledge. He could read in Latin and Greek. He was an old hand at ancient history and talked of the Romans and Greeks, Atlantis and the universal myths. And of the Aztecs. And he was, of course, a great authority on the arts and classics.

He had a remarkable mind, creative and original, and he liked to talk. The tragedy was that his listeners had lesser abilities and were usually fuzzy with booze. He should have chosen minds to grow and widen with.

Was he frightened of something in himself? Did he need to get lost in an alcoholic haze to forget horrific memories and hatreds from his childhood? Was he afraid even of being a success? Were his stupors and disappearances, immediately obliterated from his memory, attempts at damaging his reputation and upsetting his career, so that people could call him a drunk or a madman, throwing him off the tortuous yellow brick road to stardom, into the open sewer beside it?

With a few exceptions, he unfailingly chose as companions men and women who were beneath him in intellect and knowledge. Losers and drunks, hangers-on of the worst kind, weird and sometimes dangerous idlers he'd found in pubs and dragged back to meet me. After shooing them away, I'd feed him and forgive him, at one time blaming his behavior on Vivien's corruptive hold on him. Like most young women in love, I also believed the fable that I could change his bad points and round him off into the decent, monogamous, dependable genius who felt safe in the knowledge of his own worth. But I was wrong. He would never overcome the crushing reality of having been dropped in the ashcan as a child, that nobody had given a shit about him since the day he was born—and there maybe was the root of the problem. He thought he was garbage and being a successful actor wasn't going to alter his interior opinion of himself.

Once he was faced by a brain that would take no dodging. Tony Richardson, the brilliant new boy who had conceived and directed the film *Tom Jones,* starring Albert Finney, invited Finchy and me down to Saint-Tropez, the notoriously naughty resort in the south of France. Richardson had decided that Finchy should play Treplev, opposite Richardson's then wife Vanessa Redgrave, in Chekhov's *The Seagull.*

Like most actors, Finchy preferred the screen to the theater, but common to the breed, he felt that he needed to do his stint at the live theater for reasons of tradition, discipline and downright sacrifice . . . probably to his "first mistress of all, his muse." That Dame Peggy Ashcroft, a long-standing friend and a great lady of the theater, would also be starring, as Madame Arkadin, enthused Finchy with enough courage to make the trip.

As we drove south in France, I could sense Finchy's fear of confronting one of the new men in the business. Both Tony Richardson and John Osborne, dubbed by the press as "angry young men," were interpretating the deeper social and political feelings in the country, pulling the theatrical arts out of the "Anyone for tennis?" kind of light comedy that had plagued the West End since the war. It was about time, too, and whether some shook their heads and made insulting remarks about "kitchen sink drama," these young men were to bring life back to a dying profession.

A motivated and ambitious man, Tony no doubt had thought that seeing Finchy in an informal atmosphere would allow them time to get to know each other. I wasn't at all sure they'd get on. Finchy was one of the old school, while Richardson had flipped all that traditional muck onto its back. Finchy was also surprisingly sensitive about his age, and Richardson was almost twelve years younger. Born in 1916, he was now forty-six, and it was always a dangerous subject with him, although his looks belied his age, making him appear thirty-eight, if that.

We arrived at Saint-Tropez and were greeted by Tony and a houseful of guests. Always nervous of strangers, Finchy dived for the bottle. That night at dinner he was well oiled enough to perform the "public joke man" and had the company in fits. I could sense his anxiety. This was not his type of circle. Penelope Gilliatt, herself a writer of some genius; John Osborne, a complex, deceptively unobtrusive man; the composer of the score for *Tom Jones;* the composer's wife, whose nerve endings were almost visible; one or two young men who filled spaces and seemed close to the family; and the pregnant Vanessa, who sat silent as a snow queen, rocking back and forth with her arms enfolding the fruit in her belly. During the four days we were there, she never uttered. Tony was indisputably the leader of the group. A vitriolic wit who could easily bring a victim to tears, and occasionally did, he threw spikes of sarcasm at any member he felt needed deflation.

The composer's wife seemed to be the main target on this trip. Warbling with outrage, the poor woman spent most of her waking hours atremble with hurt pride brought about by Tony's quite exquisite sarcasm. He terrified me, so I decided cowardice was the best ploy, playing the sweet, rather stupid gamine. I knew I was no match here. Allowing that I had found my safe role, Tony kept off my back and I was allowed to follow him and Finchy as they walked along the beach discussing *The Seagull.* When they stopped I hung back, like an Arab's concubine. Finchy swung his elbow higher and higher to relieve the pressure of this kind of challenge.

He was not an intellectual, preferring to "feel" things, and the diamond brain of Richardson must have cut him shockingly. In Finchy's art and the way he reached his understanding of his parts, there was a process of a special kind—a process that depended on instinct and emotion and allowed to fuse gently with his consciousness. There was no thrusting "brain work" involved. The cerebral impression that Finchy gave in all his performances came from a primeval broth of memories, feelings and utter love. The brain simply projected. Tony worked from a different angle, something new to Finchy and something I believe worried and inhibited him.

For me, the sheer power of Richardson's brain brought me to the point one day where I could no longer breathe. I felt as if I were being strangled and my lungs simply closed with panic. Osborne had a way of leaning back in his chair and regarding Richardson with a calm, absorbed expression, like a man who studies the insect before he dissects it. He seemed protected from the mental glare that Richardson generated and, perhaps like all writers, he was separating the dramatic from the intellectual for later use.

At last the day came for us to leave. Immensely relieved, I threw everything in the back of the car and to affectionate, if laconic, farewells, we departed. We set off down the coast, God knows why. I should have driven back up the hills onto the main road to Paris.

Brinking on dementia, we arrived at the small town of Antibes at nine o'clock that night. I needed a bed and some food. Peter, as usual, was in full flight and wanted to continue the adventure. Feeling like a spoil-sport, I begged him to let us find a hotel. Arguing miserably, we drove round and round the deserted little square, travelers and townspeople all indoors, safely tucking dinner away. The fear of Finchy's usual travel chaos plans enveloped me and I refused to do the ring-a-rosy again. At last he suggested we take a side turning that appealed to him. To me it looked like the gateway to Hell, but I took it. There was a hotel, incredibly seedy. In panic I asked him to look in the Guide Michelin for something a little more comfortable, perhaps a modest two star. But that wasn't his style, so we went into the awful place into a cold-stone-floored hallway where the unpleasant looking proprietor offered us a room on the fourth floor, no elevator. Of course not. The room was a two-bedded death cell, with a cold marble floor, no rug, no curtains. I thought I was too tired to care, but when I ask if I could have something to eat and the man said no, I lay down on the floor and started screaming.

It was more than a tantrum. The lid had come off. I lay there staring up at Finchy, screaming the place down. He stared back, amazed and confused. Once I had started, I couldn't stop, although I remember feeling that the noise was very loud. All the rage poured out through my considerably well-trained voice box. I'm happy to say Peter had to run down the four flights of stairs and back up again with the fellow while I continued to lie on my back and scream. A doctor also had to make the ascent and for some minutes studied in amazement this young foreign woman before he sedated me with a needle. I was soon unconscious.

Peter must have been quite efficient, because the following morning I was on a flight back to beloved London. That night under the kindly and understanding care of our dear doctor, Stephen Blaikie, I was under deep sedation, where I remained for two weeks. This exceptional treatment was the same Peter had enjoyed after the long strain of trying to play Caesar to Elizabeth Taylor's forever-absent Cleopatra some years before, and I do heartily recommend it to anyone who can afford the time, like Rip and Sleeping Beauty. When you return to the land of the living, you find not much of it has changed and you can get back to making the same mistakes, with a little help from your friends. Just as if you'd never been away, and, after all, Heaven can wait. There are times in life when body and mind can't take it and something's got to give. With God's merciful intervention, something does.

Another of Finchy's streaks and perhaps the hardest to live with was an absolute determination at times to stay awake at all costs. He resisted sleep like a child, but with almost total success. After dinner and nightclubs on the town, for example, we would get home and I would make for bed, my eyes like fried eggs and my body a trembling jelly. It was always such a long day with Finchy. But not for him.

As I lay there, willing him to pass out, he would gather sheets of paper and spread them on the floor at the bottom of my bed. Collecting glasses of water, pen and pastels and water colors, he would begin to paint, finger fashion with the latter. If there were no paints, he would use ketchup and Worcestershire sauce, Benedictine, beer, toothpaste, lipsticks and boot polish. A happy twisted smile on his mouth, he would work on mysterious and primitive landscapes, vibrant with color and vision. I wasn't allowed to go to sleep, and if I did, he'd wake me and show me some wafting Turneresque river and sky that, still wet, would drip maliciously onto my blankets. He didn't need conventional paints, he was just a great aboriginal painter, but Christ, the nights, the nights! The hours would drag by for me, as I lay dying for sleep, and Finchy painted till dawn, as awake as a sunflower, with a bottle of refreshment at his side. "If I can't find the truth yet, I'll find it at the bottom of this bottle." Oh, Finchy!

As the sun rose and the bottle would empty, he'd peel an orange, flipping the skin on the carpet by the bed, drink a full bottle of milk, drop his jeans next to the orange peel and fall like a happy bohemian onto the bed, letting sleep take him for an hour. Waking, he'd turn to me, his " morning glory," rampant. These morning erections were not always welcome after another night of having to stay conscious through the hours of his creativity. To add to the injury, he'd destroy most of them the next day, unless I got there in time to save them. Really, a very destructive genius.

At last, the divorce from Tamara came through. Now we could marry, and maniac though he was, I was up to my neck in him and his life and the fantasy that once we were married, the dear boy would settle down a bit.

He wore his one and only dark suit . . . the one from *Daphne Laureola,* I think, a black knit tie from *The Battle of the River Plate,* (in the U.S. better known as *The Pursuit of the Graf Spee*) silk socks from *Simon and Laura* and the beloved pair of slip-on shoes he'd worn in every picture he'd ever made. I wore pale gray just to be safe, a Scarlett O'Hara hat to be bitchy, and handmade satin shoes, just to be extravagant!

The people of Chelsea gave us a round of applause as we entered the Registry Office, and four "old mates" witnessed the lightning event. We tripped out into the sunshine to be further blinded by flashbulbs and witty remarks from the press. "Trying to get away with a secret ceremony, Finchy? Don't want the others to know, eh? Ha-ha." The local people came around and gave us a loud ovation. It was fun.

We had seven guests to our wedding lunch at one of our favorite restaurants, The Escargot, in Soho. The menu included all the favorite things we thought our wedding should have, but each dish was something à la champagne, or a surprise à la burgundy, and so on.

I gave the ring I'd borrowed from someone back to her. Now I felt free and happy and I knew that as sure as we got on the boat to New York later that day, I'd conceive the baby my soul told me I was ready for. Finchy was beginning to make remarks about my insides, but he wasn't as anxious as I was to have a child. He felt we two were enough for one lifetime.

I was his love object and that's what I wanted to be then. I hadn't forgotten he'd told me he liked his women to be simple, and the thinking, developing woman that I became was still in infancy. When this woman did assert herself, I couldn't cope either with her or with Finchy, but I was damn sure one of us would have to be killed off.

But on that wedding day, July 4, 1959, as we received that "bit of paper" that legalized our affair, I hadn't any idea that another person existed inside my head.

10

BY THE TIME we got to New York, I was pregnant. I knew it wasn't seasickness, because the *France* glided over the ocean on silver skates.

After five days, we sailed past the Statue of Liberty.

We were met by a host of photographers and P.R. people from Warner Brothers and posed shyly for the necessary publicity shots, Finchy answering the stock questions with his marked diffidence and charm. The next five days we spent in a "Rocky Mountain" suite at the Sherry Netherland and spent many a happy hour gazing down Fifth Avenue. Honeymoon on cloud seven with all the attention Hollywood could bestow on a visiting star. And by now he was a star. *The Nun's Story* had done that for him. Typically, he was later cast in *The Sins of Rachel Cade* as another jungle hero, this time, one who falls in love with a missionary nurse, in the shapely form of Angie Dickinson.

The publicity director very soon laid out how we should behave:

"Listen, Mr. Finch." No one had called Finchy Mr. Finch since he'd sold newspapers.

"I'm listening."

"Well now. Mr. Finch. Remember that you are our guest at this hotel and I mean *anything*—you only have to ask. Hollywood likes impossible stars, boy. Make yourself *impossible,* will you please? He waited, his hangdog eyes begging Finchy.

Finchy looked nervous. "What exactly do you mean?"

"Sit down, boy—er, Mr. Finch." He pulled Finchy into an armchair. "If you aren't impossible, it makes our job so much more difficult. Be extravagant, order up cases of pink Moët et Chandon, cases of Chivas Regal, caviar—you name it. Say you've got to have a chihuahua from Cartiers; tell me you hate the suite. Be as impossible as you can. They love cunts in the front office out there. Now, will you do your best? I want to see the biggest bill we've ever had at the studios when you leave here. Get it?"

Finchy gulped. He felt sorry for the fellow. "Well, I'll try, Mr. Martin, but it's not really my style. I like simple things." The man looked as if he was going to have apoplexy. Finchy tried to calm him. "I'll do my best, really I will."

Sweating with gratitude, the man headed for the door. "Don't forget now. Anything. And I mean anything!" He threw me a glance. "Good night, Mrs. Finch."

"Cor," said Finchy. "We got it made. Now, what can we have that'll really break their backs." We both thought it over.

"Chinese?" I suggested. "We could have it sent up. That would be extravagant."

"How hungry are you, baby?" he asked me.

"Weeelll." I hesitated. "What I'd really like is a pastrami sandwich on rye with pickles and a beer."

I could see him drooling. "Do you think we could get some?"

"Have you got any cash?" I asked.

He emptied his pockets. "Should have enough here."

"Well, go down to the desk and ask where the nearest delicatessen is and buy some."

"Done."

"I'm getting in the sack."

He took me in his arms. "You keep it warm for me, baby-love."

You guessed right. Warners had the littlest bill they had ever had for a visiting fireman in New York. They were very upset and by the time we flew into L.A. we were already known as a couple of weirdies.

"Jeesus—they drink *wine*. Get it? He's a *wino!* Shit! We'll have to watch that guy like the plague. Don't let it get around. We don't want any of these kind thinking they can get away without using us! Wow! What a case! I suppose he wants to live in a nice apartment by the sea. Yeah, I thought so. What a dummy. He could have the Peter Lawson house. I'll never understand these actors. They are all—*bananas*. Mark my words, he'll be out on the next flight. Oi-yoi-yoi!"

"So where's Hollywood?" I asked Finchy as we drove through a sort of suburb from the airport.

Finchy looked puzzled. "It's here somewhere," he replied.

"I heard," I said, "that when they asked Gertrude Stein what it was like there, she answered, 'There's no there, there.' "

"Well, belt up and look at the garages," he said.

There were a lot of garages, strings of them decorated with little flags. I closed my eyes. I know when I open them I will see Frankie walking along, singing.

"Where does Frankie live?" I asked.

"Frankie who?"

"Sinatra, you fool."

"Palm fucking Springs or Las Vegas. How should I know? Now, belt up."

We moved into the Chateau Marmont, an intriguing-looking roominghouse on Sunset Boulevard. "Is *this* Sunset Boulevard?"

"Don't start," he said.

"Jesus, it's like Finchley Road with no shops or anything."

We left our tacky two rooms and went down to the pool in a small garden hedged off from the street. I was amazed. A lot of bronze creatures were lying around. None of them looked at us. I hoped we weren't going to stay long.

After a week, we moved into a nice apartment in Brentwood, near the palatial home of Finchy's producer, Henry Blanke. Henry had made such a deal with Warners back in the twenties that they couldn't break his contract until after he was dead. A real smart cookie and sweet as pie. He loved Finchy, thought he was a great actor and did everything to make us feel we weren't as strange as we felt.

"I start shooting tomorrow. Want to come and see the studios?"

"Oh, they do have studios here, then!"

The studios—Paramount, Twentieth, Warners and M.G.M.—were out of town over a hill in a sort of desert basin. We were made a fuss of and we met Angie, a pretty, long-legged girl with an angelic nature. She was in love with Blake Edwards, the director. I felt relieved.

We spent almost eight months in Hollywood and in all that time I never found it. One night I lost my cool. We were driving along the elusive Sunset. Finchy was beside me with a bottle of tequila, which had become our favorite tipple, lethal though it was. Our favorite barman, a blue-black from the South, who cooked spareribs on hickory wood—Finchy called them "angel's wings"—told us that tequila was made out of cactus leaves and had a bit of L.S.D. in it. I guess that's why after three tequilas we lost the use of speech.

Finchy had rented a yellow Cadillac for me. He had never learned to drive, although in most of his pictures you see him taking off fast in some vehicle or other. I had a sneaking suspicion that he really could drive and just couldn't be bothered.

Well, we were sailing down old Sunset again looking for Frankie and Dean and Marilyn—you know, the gang. Nobody walks in Hollywood, but on Sunset you did see groups of groupies, little Lolitas with their ponytails and jeans, drifting aimlessly about, looking for something, too. Lena Horne was playing in one of the clubs.

"Let's go see her," I said.

Lazily, Finchy took another swig. "Why?"

I stopped the car and turned to him. "What do you mean, 'Why?' She used to be a big star, you know."

"Exactly!" said Finchy.

I started a slow burn. If I was going to have to be in this asshole burg, I wanted to see action. Frank Lloyd Wright, the great architect, had described Los Angeles like this: "If you took the map of the United States of America and shook it, everything loose would fall down on L.A."

I was beginning to feel how right he was, but I still wanted to see it, loose bits and all the rest. Finchy was bored stiff.

I started the car again. "So, this is Sunset Strip, right?"

"You said it."

"You and I are driving along Sunset Boulevard where all the stars come out to play, right?"

"Oh, for Christ's sake!"

"If you don't show me Hollywood tonight and all the stars, I'm going to kick you right out of the car."

He turned up his collar. "So throw me out."

I opened the door and gave him a shove. Finchy, the agile, landed on his feet, got up on his toes for balance and twinkled down the hill and out of sight. I kept going. Stupid ass, I thought. We should be dining with Spencer Tracy or Bogarde. He is hopeless socially. Always wants to do things on his own. Let him go. Suddenly I stopped the Cadillac. I couldn't just leave him like that! Somebody would kidnap him or kill him or something else terrible. Oh, my darling. I looked around. He was gone.

"Finchy!" I yelled. Silence. "Finchy, you come back here at once. Do you hear me? At once." Nothing. I got out of the hideously unnecessary automobile and started to walk backward toward where he had disappeared. I was nearly crying. No sign of him. I looked down the steep slope that falls away on one side of the Strip. It was black and silent. Oh my God, what have I done to my beloved? I started to feel sick. Tequila and babies don't make a good cocktail. He must have gone off without me. Crying now, I got back in the car and drove home followed by two suspicious cops.

I went to bed and waited, terrified that I'd be called and told that Finchy's body was now cold in the local morgue. What a godforsaken hole this was. At last I passed out, comforting myself that sleep is always the best remedy and tomorrow would be another day.

The loved one appeared, a little dazed, at dawn, mumbling. I tucked him in.

"Where were you, my angel?" I asked him when he woke fresh as a daisy.

"I twinkled down that hill, y'know, where you pushed me out, and landed in an empty car lot on me face. Had a lovely snooze. Cold as a polar bear's asshole, I can tell you, matey."

As the film progressed, we were invited to many dinners and parties. We met some important people, but not many. Billy Wilder, Shirley MacLaine, David Selznick and Jennifer Jones, Hitchcock, but not Sinatra or Marilyn. The social game was weird and, we thought, a little provincial. For example, after a dinner party, the men would huddle together over priceless collections of pornography and the women would settle down at the other end of the room and talk about children, servants and the other usual stimulating garbage that once obsessed ordinary females the world over.

The only real kick I got in all those months was watching Natalie Wood's belly grow in size along with mine. We had the same gynecologist.

Rachel Cade was never a great picture, although Finchy and Angie gave it all they had. Too much a copy of *The Nun's Story,* in which Audrey Hepburn and Finchy had excelled. The film business is funny that way. They repeat themselves like the people who make the same dish friends enjoyed at dinner the last time.

Between bouts of throwing up—I wasn't such a natural incubator as I'd thought and had to give up smoking and drinking—I went after a couple of parts in Westerns and had a memorable meeting with Alfred Hitchcock, who asked me why I wanted to act. I should have replied, "Because it's so nice when it stops" or something witty like that. He was charming and we talked about the English weather; I flattered him and pleaded for the chance to work for him, my eyes glazed with concentrating on keeping down what was in my stomach. I gagged as I made for the door. I didn't get the part. After that, I decided to settle for knitting itty-bitty things that I never finished and that were always yellow.

Finchy behaved quite well, considering, never quite showing his distrust of Hollywood or the bitterness he felt about his last experience there with *Elephant Walk* and what he insisted was the studio's fuck-you attitude toward actors. He went to Hollywood only three times in his life; *Rachel Cade* was the second time, and *Network* the last.

We stayed for eight months. It seemed one hell of a long time and I wanted to see Big Sur, where Henry Miller lived, or even hike out to Vegas and see all the crazy money. Instead, we made it to Santa Barbara, lunched at Walt Disney's and had a distant view of Marion Davies' house from a fish restaurant on a pier somewhere. The rest of the time, while Finchy was doing his best at the studio, I spent contemplating my navel and wondering when it was going to touch my nose.

Back in New York we lunched at Sardi's and took in as much theater as we could. Finchy never went to the theater in London. What did he need to know?

II

WHEN WE GOT BACK to London, Finchy started to stuff himself with potatoes and pasta to attain the memorable proportions of Oscar Wilde, whose tragedy was to be filmed by Ken Hughes. *The Trials of Oscar Wilde,* starring snake hips, hardly seemed typecasting, but Finchy took the part with tremendous enthusiasm. Portraying the plagued homosexual poet and playwright would give Finchy a chance to express on screen his immense sensitivity and personal grace and also to challenge the world's right to destroy a superb artist for his sexual deviations. As Finchy was wont to do, he submerged himself in the works of the man, letting the soul of Wilde penetrate the deepest layers of his psyche.

The fact that another studio was perparing another Oscar Wilde film, starring Robert Morley, never gave Finchy pause. By the time shooting had started, we looked like the fat couple from the circus.

He also tried very hard to fall in love with John Fraser, playing Bosie, the cause of Wilde's destruction. He spent as much time as he could with John, a beautiful man and a superb actor, holding his hand and trying to flirt with him. One day they were in a taxi on their way to lunch in Soho. Finchy had taken John's hand and was rubbing it. John should have said, "Stroke it, Finchy, don't *rub* it. It's not sexy!" but he didn't want to be a spoilsport and I suppose he knew what Finchy was about.

"I'm trying to feel it, mate, lover, I'm trying to feel it—in here." He covered his heart with his hand. He kept rubbing. "Or even here." He pointed to his tool. Anywhere. "I want to feel obsessed by you, beloved . . ." He stared into Johnny's eyes. "I'm really trying, mate, 'cause you're beautiful." He dragged his eyes away from John's and glanced out of the cab window. "But," he said, "I keep seeing one of those!" and his lusty eyes would follow some diaphanous miniskirted dolly bird.

Finchy innocently encouraged insinuations that he was really a closet queer. He greeted old "mates" with a ritual that was dangerously close to the sort of performance an aging duchess would give on discovering a former lover on the same raft after a shipwreck. His friends did him the honor of playing along. Upon seeing each other, the two men would throw wide their arms and stand, one leg forward, like musketeers. The silence would hold the present audience in suspense for a few seconds, and then, in unison, the men would bound toward each other shouting, " 'Allo, you cunt!" and meet with a formidable *thud* in each other's arms, whereupon would follow a great slapping and kissing of cheeks and twirls of happiness around each other. Strangers watched in wonder, suspicion, and fascination until the men completed the ritual with a few more affectionate thumps and overloud cries of "Ooooo's the biggest cunt in the world?" answering simultaneously, "You, you cunt." They would then get down to the serious business of drinking and talking about their women.

Finchy would also sometimes dance with his friends. Dainty, twinkling little dances, almost Grecian, going round and round like a shepherd boy on some far-off hilltop, his eyes bright and young, as if he had fallen in love with some forest sprite. He would purse his lips and blow his invisible flute, eons of time and space behind his softly drooping eyelids and wise-happy mouth. It was as if he had known other times and histories and was now only here for a little while and for the beer. He is a mischievous creature. In his way, a sort of fairy.

One night while we were making love—and it wasn't easy: I was very pregnant—he asked me if he could put on my long black mesh chorus-girl stockings.

"Why?"

"Because I want to try and feel like a girl."

"Why?" I asked again.

"Because Oscar was feminine, you know, a sort of girl."

"Well, go on, then," I encouraged him. "Put them on."

He struggled manfully to drag them on and stood up, naked, his hands on his hips.

"How do I look?"

"All straggly," I answered. "And besides, your seams are crooked. You'd make a bloody terrible drag artist."

"Perhaps Oscar didn't drag up in girls' clothes?"

"Well, if he did, dear, I'm sure he wore something very chic. You look like a sailor's nightmare to me."

Finchy had as little atmosphere of "the feminine" about him as a bull walrus, but internally, because of his great sensitivity to the arts, he probably had quite a lot.

Ripe for our various roles, I entered a small nursing home in Welbeck Street for the birth of the child, and on the same day, Finchy began on the set as Oscar Wilde. If nothing else, the issue of our dreams started simultaneously.

Nobody had ever told me, in graphic detail, how much it *hurt* to have a baby. I'd even spoken to a mother of seven who claimed to have had an orgasm every time. I wasn't counting on that exactly; in fact, I preferred the notion that it would be something rather ethereal and spacy. Creating man in God's image seemed sufficient. However, I soon discovered that because Eve had partaken of the pomegranate in the Garden of Eden, shattering our perfect future, our outraged Lord had punished her well and good. Without going into details about cervixes and passages too small, I couldn't get Samantha to enter the world from the place she was meant to. For twenty-four hours we both did our best. I nearly asphyxiated her and it damned near destroyed me. Finchy had suggested that I should train with a hypnotist for a week or so before the arrival, in case anything unforeseen should occur. Collingwood-Entrails, or whatever his name was, was a puerile, idiotic young man and totally incompetent. Never once did I sink away into the deep sleep he would insist on my attaining; I'd simply watch his stupid bald skull and slowly swinging watch, thinking what a load of shit the whole thing was. The idea of having the fool train me to mind control the pain had been Flavia's, but the gynecological Houdini couldn't open my womb and at the twenty-fourth hour, I made such violent strangling motions at him, that the other doctors got the point about my feelings toward him and sent him away.

Finchy was, of course, down at the studios. But he was also very busy trying to get a huge "Welcome" card ready for Samantha to read when she got out. The message had drawings of storks and flowers and angels and Christ-knows-what and was signed by the entire population of the film. It was a very busy card and, I must say, a sweet thought. When the baby did arrive, one of the wittier members of the crew wrote: "What kept you so long, baby?"

Apparently Finchy was now overjoyed at the idea of the event and, in between stints at being sublime on screen as Oscar Wilde, talked of nothing but me and the baby. He didn't care what sex it was, either, an attitude that does lighten the burden for a woman. One always imagines the cowboy walking away from the doctor after being told his wife has just produced a beautiful baby daughter, a look of disgust on his craggy face.

After the Caesarean, during which, with the help of massive doses of drugs, I was mercifully absent, poor Sam, there she was—a beautiful little girl. The first thing I asked the doctor as I came around was: "Has she got all her fingers and toes?"

"All you women amaze me," he said. "You never ask if it's got a head or seven legs! Fingers and toes! Really! What a conditioned bunch of fillies you are."

Finchy was informed by telephone that his daughter had all its fingers and toes and he was so overcome with delight that he demanded that every single human being at the studio celebrate her arrival with a drinkie on him. He was over the moon with happiness and whiskey, so getting to Welbeck Street to tell us took some little time. One can see he was torn between two obligations: one, to insure that everyone knew and had a drink, and two, to get to us as soon as possible. The first obligation won.

He was pissed as a newt by the time he arrived and I was cross with him.

Almost squeezing Samantha to a pulp, which she resembled anyway, he said: "I knew it was happening, lovey. I felt all weak with terrible pains in my stomach."

I nodded sympathetically.

"I had to lie down—the cramps were ghastly! Terrifying! I never want to go through it again!"

"Are you all right now, my darling?" I asked.

"Exhausted! But she's lovely, isn't she?" He kissed her and looked so happy.

"And you're not sorry she's not a boy?"

Finchy stopped rocking, as if he'd been struck. "What?" he said, his jaw dropping. "It takes a man to make a girl, mate!" and smiled his wicked smile.

Derri Quinn, a writer friend, popped in to see us all and I watched the chortling and chucking under Sammy's tiny chin. Men are very sweet with babies, I thought. And so they damn well should be. It's easier making them than having them. Ah well!

Derri dropped Finchy off at the Savoy after they left me. The last sight he saw of the old boy was Finchy hurtling through the revolving doors, twice, to make sure, and then light-footing it backward across the lobby with his fingers in the air while he grinned like a Cheshire cat.

I spent a couple of weeks milking myself dry for Samantha and waiting for Finchy and friends to come and play with us. The picture was going well and Finchy was concentrating his considerable talents on the story of the ill-fated Wilde. Sometimes he could hardly stop his flow of tears at the sad fate of the man and he used to read *De Profundis* to me while I suckled Samantha. Some nights, unwinding at the bar at the Pinewood Studios held him up, but I understood how he felt. It got tedious only if some of his less amiable entourage insisted on accompanying him to "see baby." Finchy also had an obsession about the two cement lions that graced the front entrance to the studio. On many occasions he'd arrive, to the dismay of nurses and patients alike, huffing under the weight of one of the stone animals.

"Do you have to, Mr. Finch?" inquired matron time and time again.

"I don't know what gets into me, sir," Finchy used to apologize, "but I just can't keep me hands off them sometimes."

"Well, I wish you wouldn't bring them in here. I mean, we've got Princess Alexandra."

"Sorry," he'd say. "I won't do it again."

But he would.

The Rank Organisation got a bit miffed about it. Eventually they had the lions cemented down. When Finchy tried to lift one up one evening, he couldn't.

"Christ," he said, "they're getting heavier every day. Must give up smoking."

Rumors about which Oscar Wilde picture would be better were rife in the business. The Morley picture seemed the favorite, for the incredible reason that at that time the subject of homosexuality was a sensitive one to the British. When almost every public school boy had experienced his first love affair at school, it seemed slightly hypocritical that the public reacted as they did, but there it was. The feeling was that if a funny man played a queer, it was all right, falling with jokes about mothers-in-law's bloomers. Robert Morley was a funny man, even though he didn't play the role for comedy. Finchy played Wilde with a touch of genius. When the picture appeared, the reviews for his performance were lyrical and *The Trials of Oscar Wilde* pulled in awards from far and wide, as did Finchy, but the public really didn't want to see the story: " 'Ee was a pouf, y'know! Well, one doesn't want to see that, does one, dear? Got enuff of me own problems!"

One of the awards was, surprisingly, given by Moscow. Finchy and Ken Hughes and a few of the cast decided they should go there and receive it personally. For some little reason I didn't go along. Baby-bound.

The group was away for about ten days, during which time I gathered from informants that pretty Russian interpreters were working hard at cementing East-West relations. People said Finchy was just enjoying the caviar and vodka. Finally they flew back.

Clutching his award and a bunch of wilting Russian spring flowers to give me, he hurried off the Russian Aeroflot at Heathrow Airport. He was immediately separated from the others and escorted to a special room for a friendly interrogation.

"How did you enjoy the U.S.S.R., Mr. Finch?"

"Great place, mate. You must go there."

"Would you like to tell us about it?"

"The vodka's bloody marvelous!"

"And the people?"

"Loveliest people I've ever met."

Pushing back of chairs and lighting up of cigarettes. Pause.

"Did you meet anyone of importance?"

"Well, Kenny and I managed to escape from the others one night and caught the underground. Nearly as good as old London. We met a lovely chap on there. He'd had so much vodka the stuff was pouring out of his eyes. He took us back to his place. Nice little place. Underground."

"Did you get his name?"

Finchy thought for a minute. "Nick."

"Nick?"

"Yup. Nick. Helluva nice chap. Look, why don't we have a drop of this lovely pink vodka I brought back."

The men glanced at each other. "Not at the moment. Thank you, Mr. Finch."

Finchy was swaying amiably. The men realized that their subject for interrogation was not going to be able to give them anything very interesting, and after admiring his bunch of flowers, they let him go.

By the time he got back to Sydney Street, he was impressed beyond measure.

"They thought I was a spy, Yo! Put me through the third degree."

"They should have put you through the breathalyzer test."

We hugged each other.

"And here's a lovely present for you. Spring Russian flowers!"

"How lovely, darling. Where's the caviar?"

He looked momentarily downcast. "Caviar? I didn't think you'd want caviar, but here's two little Russian dolls. I called them Len and Grad—Len-'n-grad! Get it?"

The next morning there was a car parked outside Sydney Street with a couple of serious-looking men sitting in the front seat. Finchy was descending the front steps very carefully with Samantha in her Harrods Queen model dark blue pram. We were about to trundle off down the King's Road to show her off. He reached the pavement and negotiated the turn as one of the young men opened the car door and approached him.

"Morning, Mr. Finch."

Finchy stopped short. He looked surprised. "Yes?"

"Could we have a word, sir?"

"Well, I'm just taking my baby for a little walkie."

The man peered inside the pram.

"Nice little feller."

"It's not a feller. It's a girl."

"Whoops, sorry, sir."

"You can walk with us if you like." Finchy smiled at the young man. "And tell us your problem."

The man swallowed. "I'm Inspector Evans, Special Branch, sir." He coughed. "I'd prefer not to walk your little girl this morning, sir. If you don't mind. Nothing personal."

Finchy didn't know what the hell he was talking about. "Well, spit it out, then."

"Could I have a few words with you? In private? Sir?"

"Well, of course, old man. Come inside." He pushed the pram to me. "I'll catch you up at the pub."

I watched them disappear back into the house and Samantha and I began with our promenade. I guessed it had to be something to do with Russia, but if it was, they were sure on the wrong track. As sure as God made little apples, Finchy was just not spy material.

A friendly chat began back home.

"We hear you were very friendly with the Russian people, sir."

"I told your chaps last night. They're a lovely lot, the Ruskies."

"It's been insinuated that you were 'over' friendly."

"What's that supposed to mean? It wasn't me that was screwing the guides, mate."

"Do you have any 'political sympathy' with the U.S.S.R.?"

Even for Finchy, this was getting beyond a joke. "What exactly are you trying to suggest, mate?"

"Are you a Communist, Mr. Finch?"

Finchy let the question hang in the air for a minute. Then he spoke. "I'll tell you one thing, young man. Anyone who reaches the age of forty and didn't consider becoming a Communist is not worth knowing."

The special detective had got out his notebook and was licking his pencil.

"Don't bother to write it down, Inspector," said Finchy. "George Bernard Shaw said it a long time ago." He patted the young man on the shoulder. "Don't be upset, mate. You can't win 'em all. Relax and we'll have a drinkie."

Special Detective Dick Evans became a fixture. He'd had his orders, I suppose, to survey Finchy for a few weeks, so we decided to let him join the family. It was cold sitting outside in the car for hours at a stretch.

He learned a lot about show business, and Finchy learned a lot about the spy business—it might come in useful one day for a part. After about a month, I was fed up with Evans, who was now considering giving up his trade and becoming an actor. Finchy tried to talk him out of it.

"It's not the easiest of careers, mate. You can starve at this one and you have to be a bit of a vagabond, see? Well, you're not, are you? I mean, policemen just aren't, are they?"

The *Morning Star,* London's very own Marxist newsrag, had started making its appearance through the letterbox every morning. Finchy leafed through it a couple of times and threw it aside.

"Bunch of fuckin' nutters!" was his comment.

I began throwing Evans out in the early hours of the morning. He always looked terribly hurt when I did this, but I thought he was overplaying his part as Finchy's shadow. He'd make a lousy actor, anyway, having no real sense of intrigue or the wonder of things.

He almost cried when Finchy told him he couldn't go to the studios with him, explaining that it wasn't nice for an actor to have a bleedin' copper round his neck all the time, and anyway, Evans wouldn't want people to think he was a poof, would he? Special Dick held off for a while, but came back in full force later when in early 1962 we moved to a different house.

12

FINCHY WAS CHOSEN to play Caesar to Elizabeth Taylor's Cleopatra. His salary was doubled, bringing him up into the six-figure bracket and assuring him a place among the international stars. That was not his reason for deciding to do the picture. As usual, money did not motivate him, but playing the great general, statesman and writer did. And, of course, he liked Elizabeth and was proud to be playing opposite her.

Everyone in show business knows that "Cleopatras" have always been ill-fated. Numerous other attempts had failed and certainly the Queen of the Nile had put her hex on Britain's last film version, ironically, for Finchy, starring Vivien Leigh, along with Claude Rains. That Gabriel Pascal production had run the gamut of disasters.

The new version, a production by Twentieth Century–Fox, seemed foolproof with Elizabeth, Rouben Mamoulian, a respected and experienced director, Finchy and Stephen Boyd, a rising star with irresistible good looks and talent, as Anthony. And, it seemed, money was no object. The picture was budgeted at a cool $14 million, a modest estimate, as it turned out. It finally cost a hot $22 million and didn't get it back, either.

Finchy was indeed happy to play a man of whom he had considerable knowledge and for whom he felt great respect. Very few people realize that Caesar was a poet as well as an historian.

Finchy had studied him well. The superstitions that Cleo generated did not appear to worry him.

"Haven't you heard any knocks yet?" I asked him one day.

"No, mate. The picture will go. I feel good about it."

His instincts let him down badly. From start to finish, *Cleopatra* was everybody's special ball-breaker. Never before in the history of the film industry had a movie wreaked the sort of havoc this one was going to.

The production was to be filmed at the Pinewood Studios, and the sets, rumored to be of the greatest proportion and magnificence, were under contruction. With a cast of thousands, the costumes alone took an army of workers. Elizabeth's costumes were to be made in Hollywood.

She arrived with husband Eddie Fisher and moved into her suite at the Dorchester. Finchy was summoned to see her and I went along, also. Like most female screen stars, she is much smaller than she appears on film. The camera magnifies the figure, which is why diet is essential before shooting. Elizabeth does a crash diet of raw eggs.

Eddie appeared to worship Elizabeth and had just presented her with a sensational emerald necklace and earrings. She had laid them on the pillow in her bedroom for viewing. Girls like Elizabeth and Sophia Loren take seriously the song "Diamonds Are a Girl's Best Friend." I've come to agree with them.

Never a well woman, Elizabeth was already suffering from some illness, although at this stage, she seemed fit enough. Finchy was going out to Pinewood every day for his fittings and all seemed well.

One evening when we were over at the Dorchester, Elizabeth had a call from Darryl Zanuck. We gathered around in horror as the producer of the picture insulted his star with a sequence of obscenities such as I'd never heard. The dissension concerned money, naturally. Elizabeth was still under contract to Twentieth Century–Fox and her salary was virtually the same as it had been for the last ten years. Rightly, she was complaining. There was no chance she could win against such a big studio, but she was doing her best. She decided to let them feel some pain in return, and that's when she started not turning up on the set.

Then came Elizabeth's emergency tracheotomy at the London Clinic and she was seriously ill for weeks. The picture waited on her. Finchy was getting desperate: Mamoulian was fired. It was chaos. For nine months the farce continued.

When we visited Elizabeth in the hospital, I couldn't resist asking one of the nurses if she always looked so beautiful. "Even in the morning?" I inquired.

"Look," said the nurse, "we have a watch on that lady twenty-four hours a day. None of us has ever seen her looking anything but exquisite. Even in the morning. It doesn't seem to rub off on her pillows. It makes us mad."

But they liked her and she was and is one nice lady with a face made in heaven and the violetest eyes God ever created.

Good old journeyman actor Finchy carried on in his leather leggings, armored breastplate, sword and helmet along with all the other actors, sitting disconsolately beside the mockup Nile and playing poker. They waited and waited.

One night after another long day of nothingness, Finchy was huddled over a dish of oyster stew. Sitting beside him, I looked up to see great balloons of tears dropping into his soup. He made no sound, just the echo of the *plops* that fell from his eyes.

"Are you all right, darling?"

He shook his head, throwing a little spray in my direction.

"I'm getting a doctor," I told him.

When Dr. Stephen Blaikie arrived, he took Finchy in his arms. "I think the boy has had enough."

Unresisting, Finchy was led upstairs, where he accepted the sedation. Stephen put him in a private nursing home in Kensington and gave him sleep treatment for ten days. After that, he was fully recovered, but by then Elizabeth refused to go on . . . she was too ill, anyway, and another shot at *Cleo* bit the dust.

Finchy went on to make *Girl with Green Eyes* in Ireland. To shut me up I was given a small part. The rest of the time I played Mother and wrote melancholic poetry, never quite conquering the rhythm of the sonnet. Finchy would try to assist. Peter O'Toole was around, helping us feel no pain. I suspected Edna O'Brien, who had written the book and script, was trying to make a play for Finchy, so I was jealous, both of that and the fact that she had accomplished something on her own.

After *Girl with Green Eyes,* Finchy was drowned with offers. Producers said he was hopeless because he'd never bother to read them; he left that to Auntie Ollie, who ran our lives anyway. We decided to split for Jamaica in the Caribbean. Naturally, to find a farm. I didn't care as long as we could get out of the nothing where I was and have a go at getting back into my sexual stride, which had diminished considerably since the birth of Samantha.

It got easier after a few weeks on the beach and soft nights, yummy rum punches, smiling, singing people and the primal healing powers of the azure sea. I was beginning to function. Finchy was always functioning and searching for his dream piece of land. We first decided to buy a little island across from Ian Fleming's house, but on second thought:

"How do we get home at night?" I asked, although I was enchanted with the idea.

"We swim, you tit."

"With Sammy on a papoose tied to my back?"

"I'll carry her."

"Wouldn't a little raft be safer?"

"Ummmmm."

We sat on the little island for one whole day, playing under the trees and among the flowers and surfing and cooking a hand-caught fish over a campfire. Finchy was great at outback cooking, he'd done so much of it with his billycan . . . with the great moon . . . hanging . . . , etc. We planned to build the shack there and in the mornings we would swim across the seventy feet to the mainland and walk to the village a mile away to buy food at the market. Well, can you imagine! A pretty little land snake slithered across Samantha's foot. "Quite harmless," said father. We knew we should have the island. We wanted that little space.

"Let's buy it, then," I told him. "I bet we can get it for a bunch of bananas and if it doesn't work out, we can always sell it for two, to the local leper colony or geriatrics or something."

"It might be expensive."

"Are you crazy? Who'd buy a place like this?"

"It could be paradise," he remarked hopefully.

"And it could be hell?"

"Ummmm."

We bought a magnificent piece of land up in the hills above St. Ann along the north coast, from a Canadian millionaire whose wife didn't want to be so far from the sea. Don loved Jamaica because he believed—and so did we—that Jamaica had cured him of multiple sclerosis and he'd chosen Bamboo as his future home, planted bougainvilleas and started to cantilever a stone flower garden out over the knob of the estate, so that in it the swimming pool would hang out above the sea three miles away and give us a view of thirty-six miles of horizon. What an exquisite place it was. He gave it to us for £6,000, all twenty acres of it. Said he'd rather have lovely people like us enjoy it than some Canadian fart with money who wouldn't be able to appreciate it. Finchy balked at the price. I insisted and we bought it, both names at the bottom of the sale document.

We planted lemons and oranges and more flowers and were given a pair of peacocks and discussed where the house should be . . . near the ancient Spanish grave or next to the Indian Arawak stone? Dreams, again, all dreams. It belonged to us, yes, but on our return to London, Finchy and Auntie Ollie asked me to remove my name from the document of ownership to help him . . . tax reasons, you know, Yo dear. Like the ass I was, I did. That little place would have been nice for Charles and Samantha. It took a little time for the implications to sink in, but when they did and I realized that I'd been a fool, I began to hate Finchy. You couldn't hate dear old Auntie Ollie, could you? I mean, she was only an agent!

After our three-month sabbatical, we returned to London. I

didn't feel quite the same way about things—my man, my maternal instincts, my future, the lot. The baby had an Ibithen nurse called Eulalia, whom I'd brought from the previous nonacquisition on Ibiza, but at least she was ours and she loved us. They had their own nursery setup, built downstairs, and Finchy and I tried to recapture the old days of love before marriage. Finchy's need to be reassured that he was loved always settled in the region of his genitals. Cock satisfied, he would put up with anything, even open hostility. Without a regular diet, he got disoriented and ego-shocked. We'd been together four years now and I wasn't quite the abandoned fuck-rabbit he'd got used to. He was still behaving like an aging Lothario; of course, in his time, according to his discovery of Mother, he was still only eighteen or so emotionally. When he got cross with me for saying no, I don't want it, he'd rush off to Ma's or the "wild wetters." One night, he got back so late—this was in the early stages—that I locked him out of the house. He took a bit of a stroll and ended up in Hyde Park on a bench with a tramp who gave him half his newspapers to keep him warm. The next day Finchy told me in a melancholy voice, "It's at times like that, that you know who your real friends are." Another time, somebody's ex-wife was in the house next door, using the ground-floor room to sleep in. She was exceedingly surprised when her window was quietly and surreptitiously opened and suddenly a figure appeared clambering through the window to fall on top of her in bed. The figure looked around. "Christ," he said, "I've got the wrong house."

"Pity," she remarked, realizing who he was, and he clambered out again.

Incidents like these were not frequent, and when he came back, he looked sheepish rather than roguish.

"Where the H have you been?"

"I don't know. I got lost."

"In what?"

"I don't want anybody but you, Yo. I love you."

"I love you, too, but you're such a mess."

"I'm sorry. I do love you."

"I should give you more."

"No. It just gets me sometimes and I run away and hide."

"But where, my poor love?"

"I don't know. Wherever they find me, I suppose."

"My poor baby."

He'd sleep a little and then I'd ask him, "Where'd you hear about—I mean, where are the 'wild wetters,' darling?"

He'd close up. "Don't know. Something about Kipling. Don't know. We'll be all right, Yo. Stick with me."

It was killing me the way he was trying to destroy himself. I was beginning to withdraw and I knew I shouldn't, for the simple reason that he needed me, needed to be loved in spite of anything he did. He craved reassurances and acceptance and I was too young to give all that energy to a man who should have learned by now that what you give, you get. And Finchy never gave his truths or his secrets or even token gifts that didn't need words. A red rose isn't an adequate substitute, but it is a soft denial. When two people are lovers, there are certain intimacies, confidences that have to be shared. Questions never asked or never answered make a profound silence that even a million orgasms can never fill. I stopped kissing him on the mouth and we began to be just simply a double-backed beast in sexual combat where there was no real beginning to us and no foreseeable future. It's called The Beginning of the End.

We were entertaining pretty regularly. The house had a sweetness and drew friends and hangers-on alike. I usually invited the friends, and Finchy incited the enemies, the earthbound: "Come on, Finchy, you can't go to bed now, mate! It's only five A.M.!"

I liked having parties and tried to protect both of us from the dregs. He'd started another picture, called *No Love for Johnnie,* for producer Betty Box at Pinewood, with Ralph Thomas directing. Incidentally, they *discovered* Raquel Welch as they did Brigitte Bardot. A couple of youngish promising actresses and one real pro actress supported him in the story about a politician—one of the cinema's surefire audience repellents. As usual, he was marvelous and picked up awards left and right. The one on the right came from Berlin . . . this side of the wall. We went there and picked it up and had some disgusting *gemütlich* celebrations with other collecting artists from abroad.

Returning home, I realized that Samantha, Finchy, Eulalia and I were just too many people, not counting haunting suicides, white horses' heads and swirling silk skirts for Sydney Street. The little house, two up and two down, was just too small for all of us. I persuaded Finchy that we needed a bigger place. After a time, Auntie Ollie agreed to buy Boundary House for us, a neo-Georgian thing in the middle of seven acres somewhere in Mill Hill, God forgive us. Mill Hill is a deadly suburb, nine miles as the crow flies from Marble Arch, Mayfair, but when you live there for a day, you realize that it's not close enough to London or not far enough away. It's one of those suburbs that you can never get to from town in less than two hours, unless you are a crow or own an airplane.

Anyway, I take the blame. I made them do it. I thought of the yellow of spring, daffodils and summer lawns and the smell of roses, country streams and paddocks where foals and their elders would leap and laze. I even thought of buying a cow and ducks. Instead, the country house was already attached to one of civilization's least attractive animal farms, the chicken battery deep in litter, an overdeveloped barracks, something along the lines of Buchenwald, which housed 2,000 embittered caged fowl, ceaselessly producing eggs and eggs and eggs, egglessly for us, because they were for the state-run egg board. Prisoners producing, until featherless carcasses were taken for something else's food. My fault, though. All my fault. I thought chicken for everyone was a fun idea.

We hadn't had a repetition of the ladies-of-the-night episode, but that didn't mean that Finchy's fantasy had passed and now that I was becoming less accessible, I wondered when he'd try it again. By now our lovemaking had, for me, become the old marriage joke: "Don't come yet—I haven't thought of anyone!" I didn't say it, but my whimpers and groans of pleasure would have pleased even Lee Strasberg. Acting the orgasm wasn't very difficult, but who was going to cast me as an orgasm?

He must have known it and it must have hurt him. He had the power to enchant both men and women. He could be a gentleman, a delightful and warm man, but something was missing. His hidden message was "Don't lean on me. I might let you fall." He had his deep needs—who doesn't?—but tragically, he couldn't express them in real life. On screen, by all means, but next to you or inside you, you were chasms away, valleys apart from each other, and the echoes were getting fainter. His deep need was to know he was loved, even if he was vile, which he believed himself to be. He loathed himself and so it was easy for him to do loathsome things. At such times, his eyes would take on that familiar faraway look, he sat moody and remote, turning up his collar, slumping down, his glass tipping the contents onto the floor. There was an anger there, a very, very, deep and dangerous anger. I could understand. I knew, but I couldn't reach him. He was a long time gone. He'd pull himself to his feet, swaying, but looking tough, and "I'm off to the 'wild wet woods.' " No pleading could stop him now if he felt he'd been rejected. And he had. By me. By the one person who should have poured oceans of love into his empty cornucopia, even knowing that at its tip, there was a terrible crack and all the love would drain.

Fiercely alone, he'd stalk off into the undergrowth for a while, spending his preciousness on a search that was never to be completed, because although he could hear the scream of pain, he tried to find its source somewhere outside him. Kipling's cat.

We had a celebration party for *No Love for Johnnie* at home at Sydney Street before we moved to the new house. It was a good party. The sixties had turned their page, and life took on a more purple hue, a wilder light. About a hundred people came, the majority of them from the business, others from Finchy's drinking holes, but it went well. The food was good and the music and drink flowed. Even I had a ball, but then I loved parties and rapping about things and there was always enough of my kind of people to play with, to keep me happy and dancing on tables. As usual, the *crème de la crème* left early. I wanted to go, too. We were getting down to the serious drinkers of both sexes. One of the Australian girls had already thrown up in the kitchen, and looking around at the mob, which included Finchy, telling one of his old jokes in the midst of a group of swaying wet-lipped sycophants, I decided to call it a day. There was no way I was going to get those fuckers out, so I took the next best alternative. I went to bed.

I was dozing off a couple of hours later; the noise was not conducive to sleep and I wondered when Finchy would throw them out and come up when suddenly, the bedroom door opened. A crumpled figure appeared, the blob on top of its shoulders grinning drunkenly. I opened my eyes and he put his hand in front of his mouth as if to stop me from making any nasty remarks. Half his body was still outside the room and in a second I saw that at the end of his arm, as he entered fully, was a woman. I recognized the woman as one of our North Country actresses, making a name for herself not only as an easy lay, but as a girl with the genuine North Country tongue very much in vogue at the time. Before I closed my eyes, I noticed that she was pissed, too, and one of her dirty white stiletto shoes had come off somewhere along the line.

I felt rather than saw them approach. A sizzling rage hovered across my forehead and images of little black-winged devils haloed around my head. "Oh God, no. Not her! She can't even act!"

"Darling? Darling, Yo? Look what I've brought for you. Yo?"

I opened my eyes as slowly as the sun would if it knew that this was the earth's last day. Oh God! She stood there lopsided, in her strapless white ruched dress, and she was giggling. He held her hand and swayed. I let my eyelashes drop over the sight, leaving a very little slit to observe through. I would pretend to be asleep and they'd go away. I saw Finchy hesitate.

"Yo? She fancies you. Yo? Wake up."

She started to struggle with the long zipper that connected the dress at the side. It stuck and, giggling, both of them fiddled until the teeth unknit. The dress slithered to the floor, and she stepped out of it, exposing the rest of the seductive gear—everyman's dream, the Merry Widow corset . . . in *black!* Under *white?* Naturally. Her tits scrunched up and her leg fat scrunched down, pulling the garters tight down to the tops of her stockings. No panties. Black pubes and blond hair. Yes, there it was . . . the other woman that would make such a beautiful picture making love to me. Was he deranged . . . blind with a memory of a time when he'd made love in the wildback when there was no moon? Was I really mixed up in some aboriginal group-fuck after a diggeridoo? Whatever the hell that was.

I slid farther under the bedclothes, still pretending tight sleep. I didn't want to turn my face . . . they would have known. I could hold everything if they would just go away.

Finchy stood in the middle of the room, fully dressed in his usual jeans, shirt open to waist and bare feet. Maidenform looked a little nervous, but not much. I watched Finchy fall out of his jeans and unbutton his only attached piece of shirt. They stood in front of me like a couple of pieces of Bowery junk . . . up for sacrifice.

"Fuck off out of my bedroom."

I said it very slowly and clearly so that they would be able to understand a human feeling through a human language.

Finchy bounded over to me.

"I knew she'd be awake. Come on."

I reared back and hissed like a fox. How little he knew how close he was to death. And yet, somehow, I was transfixed with the horrible novelty of it. What were they going to do now? What did people like this do now; to me, with me, against me? I couldn't kill him and she was meaningless, but I had to see it through, live through it, just for the sheer cruel beauty of his obsession or for the brutally existential fact that people did this all the time. It was life. Had I the right to tell them it was wrong? Had I any right, for that matter? Had any of us, and, most of all, what was wrong? My not wanting something? Dead on!

Lying there rigid, I gave it a go.

"Look, why don't you two go downstairs and have a good—"

Finchy was on top of me, his mouth gaping for kisses. I bit flesh and he pulled away, turning to the actress who'd come up beside him. She took his bloody lips and he clasped her with all his might. Just as quickly, she pushed him away and leaned over him on her elbow, "Come on, luv, it's only fun." Her common little rat's face smiled and he turned beseechingly to me. To attract people like this, I thought, I must have a spectacular spook charm. I know Finchy didn't realize that his mouth looked wounded. The way he hated raw meat would have made him run for the basin, and now she was crawling over him, making for me? Or about to mount him. In all nightmares, there's the one-millionth of a split trillionth of a second when the image gets too scary and you wake up. This was that ion of time that brought me out of the living dream.

Slowly I got out of bed. I knew I had to be very calm or else I might have killed them both with the marble statuette standing so accessibly on my bedside table. I didn't turn back as I dressed and gathered my things from the bathroom. Only once did I go near the bed, to pick up her discarded Merry Widow, and as I walked very quietly down the stairs, I threw it in front of me so that it landed *clunk* almost at the front door, the devil's emblem.

I walked across Chelsea after leaving a note in pidgin Ibithencan to Eulalia, to tell her and Samantha that I was going away for a few days. I wanted to take Samantha, but it would have been unfair in the cold dawn. Feeling quite disconnected, bumping into the dim figures of the early cleaning ladies on their way home after a night's office cleaning, I reached a friend's house, woke her and asked her to keep me until I could think of what to do.

I didn't want to go back. That was certain. He'd done this to me before, or I could, if I had tried, have pretended that that was a drunken accident. Was twice a coincidence? But I loathed him. And he now had my baby.

He looked for me for two weeks. I kept in touch with Eulalia, swore her to secrecy, and she brought the baby to me. Finchy was going frantic, crying and telephoning everyone we knew. My friend kept mum, hiding me like Anne Frank any time he or his friends came searching. As far as I was concerned, the coffin of love was nailed shut.

Sophia Loren and Anthony Perkins were to make a picture in Paris, called *Five Miles to Midnight.* I heard about it and flew there for an interview with Anatole Litvak, the director, who gave me a part. Perhaps I still had a chance to pull myself from the strangling, sinking sand of marriage. Of course Finchy had to know, because Olive Harding was my agent. Once again, the miraculous gift of amnesia had clouded his memory of why I'd gone away, but this time I wasn't going to talk about it. I told him I was taking the family to Paris to make a picture and did just that. I couldn't wait to get out of his sight.

I was third lead in the fine old melodrama, but how lovely to be sleeping alone and working. I enjoyed the passes that were made at me, but after years of being spread-eagled under Finchy, virtue was a reward.

Once again my career was short-lived. Determined, I believe, to tie me close to him, Finchy flew to Paris every weekend. I took him back . . . the sweet nature of him; the light, apologetic, shy smile; the fun and humor and, again, the beginning of love, the repetition and heaven-only-knew-what-next punishment. . . . The way things are. We lay again as lovers, on an antique French bed in the sensual daintiness of a romantic suite, reflecting our pretty selves from mirrored walls. Perhaps silence and night are enough . . . at least they are allies. Sometimes, wandering between the silk chairs, leaning against the desk, I watched him sleep, and returned beside him. The twin natures within me wrestled in sweat. He was my husband and I should have known that nothing could ever be perfect. We should go on trying . . . the child. His need of me. All that. And then the other self, more dominant now, battling for a life, with a quiet, deeper voice. Fighting for my life, perhaps alone—anyhow, against the hurt. The whispers of my own faults, weaknesses, mistakes. I subdued the deeper, inner tone. After all, he was the *man,* the genius, the achiever. I decided to play the game and found that by reversing my special gift of memory, I too could find its useful colleague, amnesia. By putting memory's face to the wall, I found her back was deaf and couldn't or didn't want a relationship with tomorrow, and the present took care of itself. Finchy needed a serene godmother, all-forgiving. He craved understanding and acceptance and I should be able to offer them to him. I was just too young for the role.

I wanted to be free of him. My returning frigidity must have terrified him and yet my resistance to him spurred him into a greater intensity, a desperate, rampant desire to turn me back onto him, and I allowed him to have me as I lay passive and thought of the luxury of reading a book alone. The colder I became, the deeper he plunged, my vulva swelling like the lips of a slave and the acid from his drinking stinging like cold ice. I lay back and thought of England, but I damned the day I had first set foot on her. I conceived.

True to form, my guts rebelled and Anatole Litvak caught me being sick on the set and guessed the cause.

"You want to ruin your career?" he screamed. "Get rid of it!"

Paris in those days was not the place to find an abortion. I bribed and begged, but it was "strictly against the law, madame." I experimented with infamously dangerous other methods. I took black pills, squirted scalding water up, jumped a lot and hurled myself down the front steps of the Hôtel Raphael. There was no shifting it. I'd had it. I finished the picture, feeling like a fool, and wrapped up my remnants of dreams for the future as a good journeyman actor like my happy husband would do. When the movie came out, I got my mention from the critics, but as far as show business was concerned, I was a dead loss.

13

THE JAPANESE BUS CONDUCTOR, as Finchy described his son, was delivered to me at an appointed date in August 1962. It was a fairly accurate description of Charles, yellow and scrunched, with anxiety etched on his face, reminding me once again that as a conveyance for the newly born I was no cinch. It took me a little while to feel anything but a distant sense of responsibility toward him, which thrust Finchy into the role of superdad. He did the cuddling this time and I left them to each other. Finchy was particularly delighted by his son, having during the months previous to his birth been in Greece to make *In the Cool of the Day,* with Jane Fonda and, while there, having taken advantage of the oracles at Delphi, who, it appears, had communicated to the inebriated actor that the child that was coming would be a genius. And a man-child. Premier Papadopoulos presented Finchy with a minute gold coin three thousand years old and told him to place it in the palm of his son after birth. This ceremony would ensure him a place among the Gods. Much impressed with myths and legends, a deeply thoughtful Finchy transferred the blessing to the Japanese bus conductor's palm at their first meeting and Charlie held fast to it. It's a pity Finchy didn't hang around long enough to see his son grow into a very extraordinary young man.

Four weeks later, we were off again, by boat to New York and on to Jamaica. Samantha and I lost pounds of flesh under the continual screams of the hyper Charles. He bawled day and night, never slept unless in someone's arms, tried to talk to anybody who would listen and sent me hysterical when, lying on my back for a little rest, I'd place him on my stomach, hoping the tidal sounds from within would woo him to sleep but instead felt him trying to crawl up my body. At four weeks! It was unreal. This child was his father's son. No doubt about that. I pitied his future women and told Finchy that if he didn't take over his monstrous progeny, I might have to throw him overboard. Recognizing something of himself in Charles, Finchy became his mainstay. They were made for each other, strolling the decks at dawn, drinking with the boys on board, singing and rolling on the floor. Samantha and I withdrew under blankets on deck, like old ladies taking the last cruise.

From New York, we took a gay little American ship to the Caribbean. As usual, our timing was beautiful. Two days out of Miami, the captain called us to hear a speech from President John Kennedy. The Russians were coming and war was just around the corner, probably starting a few miles to our left in Cuba. Everybody stood up and sang the National Anthem and then got drunk. I went to bed.

For Finchy, the eternal traveler, these knee-wobbling warnings of disaster were grist to the mill. He was not a political man, and rockets pointing at the United States were just one of life's little games, but the titillation of being in an actually fraught position while traveling fulfilled his highest expectations of the possibility of immediate extinction and made him very happy. I stayed in bed. Overhead, planes from the United States dipped and circled around us. We were under protection. Once again, everybody stood up and sang the Anthem. Finchy was beginning to like the American attitude of "We'll fight to the death," and Charles was probably learning the words. Holding Charles in his arms one evening, Finchy remarked, "Well, one thing I've learned, Yo—you can't define the whole of America by Hollywood." I turned back to Scott Fitzgerald.

Things were hotting up. We were ordered to proceed to Venezuela and dock there for the time being. A lot of passengers were aggravated at being sent away from the imminent battlescape. "I'll kill those Commies with my own hands" comments came out of the mouths of timid, retired southern gentlemen, and their women got very upright and grizzly-haired, flinging their flowered plastic bags around in aggressive arcs to emphasize their fighting spirit. Actually, they were admirable, but perhaps they hadn't noticed that we didn't have a warhead on board that week.

"Don't worry, darling," said Finchy.

"Who's worrying?" I replied, too tired to care.

"We can always buy a little farm in Venezuela."

"Oh yeah?"

"Plant some potatoes . . ."

"And plant some cotton?"

Charlie was gum-grinning me.

"And what will we do for money?" I sneered, having lived with Finchy long enough to know that he didn't travel with the stuff. Auntie Ollie always settled everything up afterward.

"We'll get Auntie Ollie to send some."

I paused at this exquisite ignorance. "Peter. There is going to be a war. Maybe." Sigh. "And if there is a war, Auntie Ollie won't be able to send any money. Peter."

His spirits lifted considerably, a huge smile breaking across his healthy tan. His son gurgled in his arms. Finchy jogged him up and down.

"Nothing can happen to us, mate. We've got him here. We're protected! We'll start a little farm and grow things and live like the real poor forever after."

I shook my head slowly, thinking that, as the saying goes, "If I didn't have bad luck, I wouldn't have any luck at all."

"Order me a double gin fizz, will you, Finchy?"

He looked disturbed. "You shouldn't have a drink now. You don't need it."

"I need it more than you'll ever know."

As expected, Venezuela was everybody's perfect setting for the end of the world. The loudspeaker boomed out the encouraging strains of our favorite tune as the passengers disembarked. There was a rather sweet-solemn demeanor about the cruise people and I found the unshakable belief in the survival of the U.S. of A. extremely touching. I wondered if we'd all end up together on a commune, ploughing the earth and making wheat cakes and moonshine. The last screams from a dying planet. Everybody calm and orderly as they drifted around the dirty port looking for taxis and smiling at an odd Venezuelan dockworker. Other ships with other stories were tied up along the quay, but the place had a deserted, sinister feeling to it.

Finchy, the children and I boarded a battered taxi to go to look for a farm. To the gold-plated grin of the taxi driver, Finchy described, in Ibithencan, his quest. I noted the two bullet holes in the windshield but didn't ask how they'd got there. With a touch of genius, the driver took us straight to the shanty town on the outskirts of Caracas. Picturesque lean-to shelters made of cardboard and newspapers littered the hillside. The man watched us through his mirror, his teeth glittering with amusement . . . or was it malice? Finchy, holding Charles, sat forward on his seat and studied the poverty. He didn't speak, but he looked puzzled. I'd seen it all before in *The National Geographic,* so it was a replay of a sickening visual I could have done without. Finchy tried to communicate his sympathy for the people to the driver, who laughed loudly. Then we drove through the great rich city to be shown the other side of the picture.

"Ask him to take us into the countryside a little," I told Finchy. "Maybe you'll see your farm."

I knew how hard it was for Finchy to face the realities of life when sober and his expression had become depressingly sad. He began to shrink back, that lonely, frightened look invading his eyes. To make it easier on myself, I hoped we could find something to take his mind off the scene and, by my unfailing method of speaking English very loudly and very slowly, told the man to get us out of the city.

As we drove away into the flat country, we saw a lonely old nag standing behind a fence. Immediately, Finchy revived. He loved horses and they loved him. They brought back memories of a life of freedom and no cares.

"Stop here, mate."

The car drew up.

"Lookie! A lovely old nag!" We all smiled gaily and made our own noise to encourage him. Slowly, he left the taxi and walked to the fence. The horse retreated.

"Come on, me old lovely. I'm not going to hurt you."

The horse looked as though he'd heard that one before and laid his ears back. Finchy approached carefully, almost on tiptoe, with his arm outstretched, his palm hanging listlessly toward the earth. He glanced back at us.

"See?" he staged-whispered. "With me palm down like this, he doesn't think I want anything." The old mad horse stepped gingerly forward.

"See?" asked Finchy gleefully. "He knows I'm not aggressive. Come on, old fellow."

We watched the animal move closer to Finchy's hand.

"Jesus, it'll have your hand," I screamed.

"Shhh! He understands. I'm defenseless with the Buddhist hand, mate. It's a signal. He knows. Just watch."

Carefully the horse began to sniff the top of his hand. Finchy's joy was overwhelming. He bent his head and gave the horse a long slurp with his tongue. The startled creature backed off for a second and gave Finchy a disapproving look.

"Come on, old boy, give us a kiss." After seconds the two of them were sniffing and slurping as if they had known each other all their lives. Finchy had that sort of emanating gentleness that even *dumb* animals found hard to resist. The next step was inevitable and even the driver's mouth dropped as we watched Finchy climb under the fence and get up onto the horse. At some mysterious signal the horse tore off into the distance, carrying the jubilant Finchy, yelling and laughing, and we watched as they flew over the red earth. Once Finchy fell off. His equestrian mate slowed up, Finchy caught his tail, and off they went again. When Finchy's arms got tired and his jeans got holes in the knees, his new buddy stopped, knowing it all somehow, and stood waiting, his head turned back toward Finchy.

Where had the fear gone, I wondered; here was a happy man, a cowboy, country boy . . . farmboy. What was he doing in the terrible, dangerous profession of acting? If anyone on earth wanted a farm, this "wild wet woods" man did.

We never found a farm that day outside Caracas, but at least one of us was highly exhilarated when we returned to the ship to hear the latest news on the war situation. The Russian warships had turned back after Kennedy's ultimatum. We all sang "America, the Beautiful" and got drunk.

Back in London again after a few weeks in Jamaica, Finchy began *The Pumpkin Eater* with Anne Bancroft. Special Evans and I moved us out to Boundary House, which, with its muddy acres, provided at least some earth for Finchy to plant his potatoes. Finchy got himself a lady's bicycle from the local ironmongers and cycled down to the village for seeds and bits of string in between studio calls. He seemed to enjoy *The Pumpkin Eater,* although he never talked about his work except that Anne Bancroft seemed to satisfy him enormously as a fellow player. I went to the location once or twice, but felt very out of things. Perhaps at this point of the game I should have started asserting myself and hanging around more until somebody noticed me again. Bloody pride and motherhood forbade it and, consequently, it might have looked to the show people that I had become domesticated, like a cow. Not enough push, my girl. Not enough push, by half.

The small holding that was Boundary House flourished. Finchy in his Wellington boots, would often be down among his cabbages and 'tatoes, standing proudly with a grim pioneering look on his face for photographers from movie magazines. Reams of trash about the hell-raising farmer appeared for besotted audiences. A gardener was hired to do the heavy stuff, although, to be fair,

Finchy did try his hand at the pitchfork occasionally. Great throbbing branches of tomatoes drooped under their weight in the hothouses, thousands of lettuces sprung forward, and the glut of cabbages, too many to pick, grew like triffids to six feet. We bought a deep freeze to try to handle the harvest and later I tried to sell the stuff to restaurants all over London. The chickens picked at one another and laid thousands of eggs, which we gathered and put through a sort of golf ball wash device to be all fresh and clean for the egg board to collect. Miraculously, we managed to run at a loss of about only £3,000 a year, and sloshing around the fecund mud with Finchy, I wondered sometimes why he couldn't, instead, have gone in for antiques, like Michael Caine. But he was happy; he was relating to the children, trying, it seemed, to play the family man.

Trying, myself, not to make waves, I wasn't hiding in the bathroom as much as I had been or pretending to be asleep when he was randy. Possibly I thought that playing the whore might get him to set up the production of *The School for Scandal* he'd been promising to do with me. We never did it. Occasionally, I forayed into the provinces on "tryouts" for London, but luck and the choice weren't there. I made it once into the West End in a play about ghosts, called *Staring at the Sun.* The critics advised the public to stay home and stare at the TV instead.

We lived in comparative luxury. I had accounts at all the shops. Finchy wouldn't be seen dead in a store, so I bought his black socks. He hated dressing up. The uniform was the blue jeans, the open-to-the-waist button-down-collar, blue ivy-league shirt and a beloved and much frayed seersucker jacket, which he'd stolen off somebody. Sometimes he'd have to go into town to see a producer or suck up to Auntie Ollie, but he didn't like it. And he'd try to get out of the house without shoes and socks. By now we had a Spanish couple, and Manuelo would wait for him at the front door and grab him as he tried to make a run to the car. "Señor Finch can't go to the city without his shoes and socks." Finchy would sit unhappily while Manuelo put them on him.

Finchy drank when he was bored and he was often bored. For a man who lived at a great pitch of intensity within himself and saw and felt things strongly, the ordinary world was a dull place indeed. I concurred, but for different reasons, and we didn't try to speak of it. He was more fun to be with when he was a little drunk, somewhere around the middle of the descent. We had many a gay night in London and many a wild party at home. Most of his drinking mates were more overtly aggressive than Finchy, who was never a man to resort to fisticuffs. I remember Finchy subduing Peter O'Toole after he'd punched through a cupboard, which I had committed the sin of shutting. Sian Phillips, Peter O'Toole's then wife, told me anything was better than divorce. I was beginning to wonder.

A great raconteur, Finchy kept hundreds of friends and lesser people paralyzed with laughter. Like many wives, I'd heard the anecdotes so often, I preferred the new ones I got from other people. Roger Moore, for instance, was a brilliant storyteller who had a new one every day. Where he got his jokes I'd still like to know. I used to work with Roger sometimes on TV and I'd spitefully recount his stories to Finchy, which made him mad. He wanted to write a screenplay about a man who's shipwrecked and makes up stories on his hammock while he's being fed love and banana punch by beautiful native girls; he finds life so pleasant and amusing that he resists being "saved" by the ships that call at the island, but he sells the sailors the stories to tell around the world. But it was night talk, like most of his best fantasies.

When my Mama hit another seven-year crack-up in South Africa, I flew off to help Daddy get her straight and left Finchy with Derri Quinn to write a screen version of a story called "The Hero," which Finchy had been driving us crazy about for months. He bought the screen rights, got Derri in to write the script with him, planned, like most actors, to direct it himself. By the time I'd got back, they had a script, but Finchy didn't have the chutzpah to get it on the road. He just sort of backed off.

But drunken stories were an upper for him and he didn't give a

SUGGEST THE AUDIBLE	SUGGEST SOUP VEGETABLE SALAD	APPETIZER FORK OR SPOON	SERVE HOST LAST	RECHECK FOOD ORDER & CHECK	USE MEMBER NAME	SUGGEST WINE

SERVED BY	TABLE NO.	MEMBER & CHAIR		TABLE NO.	SERVED BY

	COCKTAIL	APPETIZERS	SOUP	SALAD	ENTRE	VEG.	BEV.	OTHER
1								
2								
3								
4								
5								
6								

damn who the audience was. Tales of his early days in London, when the "wild wetters" meant spending the night with a few of the boys at Jerry's or Jacks in the company of the Crazy Gang; nostalgic half-truths about being a straight man to a brutal comedian in Australia; stories about a famous actress being poured into a taxi at dawn, and her drunken mates taking so long to give her address in Golder's Green that the lady gets out the other door in the belief that she has reached her destination and asks how much she owes. And about Coral Browne waving a taxi down outside the Ritz Hotel one night and getting in, only to be confronted by a man who'd approached from the other side, and saying, "This is my taxi." "No it's not. It's mine," says the misogynist, and the taxi driver says, "It's the lady's taxi." And the mysogynist remarks, "What lady?" and Coral Browne replies, "This fucking lady!" And Vivien Leigh's story about the girl on the bus with her shopping, sitting opposite a sex maniac, who is trying to look up her skirt and how when he's got his head practically on the floor for a better view, she crosses her legs and asks snappily, "Well, what does it look like now?" "Like this," he replies, and twists his mouth into the shape of a squeezed mollusk . . . funnies like that which made him laugh happily and somehow topped him up. Because the "swinging sixties" made him feel like an outsider and he didn't want to get old before he caught up. He wasn't a swinger in the modern sense of the word. Beatles were little black things you found crawling across the floor and drugs appalled him. "I'm not even taking an aspirin, Yo. It's a sign of weakness." While we were all avidly absorbing Huxley and his experiments with lysergic acid and wanting to open the doors of perception ourselves, Finchy thought the whole movement extremely suspicious. He was old-fashioned. Probably certain mysteries genuinely frightened him and he felt that some things should be left alone. Perhaps, he thought, if he had tried even pot, he would have lost hold of that iron coil that held him in a semblance of control. He even discarded music as a stimulant. He was square. It amazes me now to realize just how inhibited he was.

London had a lovely moody glow in the sixties, a ripe, adventurous, bloody-minded crusadelike energy about it. Everyone wanted to say his piece and prove that something did matter, that probably everything had a meaning; the air was thick with caring and wanting to know what it was all about. Flower people populated the parks and marched with intellectuals against the bomb and other horrors. The world was tripping out to solve the mysteries and bring them back illuminated. Kenneth Tynan told me that he only understood that all matter is alive and well and moving, when he took a drop of acid on a lump of sugar and watched the loaf of bread in front of him come to life and the chair and the wall. I enjoyed a drag of Angel Dust that turned me into Alice in Wonderland the size of your little finger and took away the power of speech for eighteen hours. But we were all seeking something in the sixties and that made the sixties worthwhile.

Sexually, the barriers were down, too. If people needed people, they had them. Not in the secret, salacious way of the Victorians, just more openly. I was jealous. I was frigid with my heartthrob hell raiser, I hadn't had an orgasm for a year and I was wondering what was the best way to tackle the problem. I needed to be loved. Feeling it would be disloyal to take a lover from among the new thinkers, I decided to call on a mutual friend of Finchy and me. Ken Hughes was delighted when I asked him to meet me at the Dorchester for a drink. I got there earlier than he did, but I didn't have to wait long.

"What is it, Yo luv?"

"Will you be my lover?"

"What?"

"Will you take me upstairs and make love to me."

"Christ, can't do that, mate. Finchy's my best friend."

"But you've always flirted with me—been nice to me—"

"I know, luv, but I couldn't. I'd love to. Truly. But I just couldn't do that to old Finchy."

"Thanks, Kenny."

I decided to fall in love with Peter O'Toole. He was terribly handsome and I thought he might turn me back into a woman. Finchy and I spent a lot of time at the O'Tooles', eating and drinking and dancing wild folk dances, but I couldn't seem to communicate my needs to Peter either.

Another couple of renown in show business brought me to my senses. I must have been getting desperate. The man was handsome enough to make a possible subject and at this stage I wasn't too concerned with the feelings of the wife, who seemed pretty free herself, so I surged ahead. We'd had a smoke and it was late. Finchy was night shooting and it seemed as good a time as any to play the seductress. I put out the heat, and wonder of wonders, the actor picked me up in his arms and carried me upstairs. He put me down on the bed and started to undress me, kissing me divine, heavenly kisses on the mouth all the while. I sank into the wonder of sensuality . . . at last, my dried-up, bitter sex was melting . . . I was becoming a soft, loving female creature again. Opening my eyes, I saw his wife slipping out of her silk evening pajamas at the bottom of the bed, then naked, walking toward us, with a lovely, soft, female smile. When I felt her mouth on me I jumped like a scalded cat. The bastard. The man had betrayed me! I shoved them both off. Slowly, she replaced me, and he began to make love to her while I sat there . . . *amazed!* I gave him a hell of a whack on the behind, which did nothing to disturb his rhythm, and left the house unnoticed and I believe unmissed, but very, very angry. When I got home I wished I'd stayed. Perhaps Finchy was right. Everybody seemed to be doing it.

Finchy was not a social butterfly by any stretch of the imagination. He disliked High Society intensely, and as I have said, anyone who had been to a public school was immediately dubbed "a chinless wonder." Sometimes he accused me of being a snob because I preferred the company of literates. Titles were anathema to him, except for the Queen herself, for whom he carried a colonial devotion.

"And they never knight poofs!"

"Like who?"

"Noel Coward."

"They will. They will."

Finchy was a wise man in some ways. He had a remarkable mind, which made the kernel of morbid escapism all the worse to bear. His extravagance was unholy, his largesse notorious. Harry Meadows, the owner of Winston's nightclub in London, wrote a letter to him begging Finchy "not to keep spending hundreds of pounds every night treating all the customers to drinks!" He went on to say he'd rather keep Finchy as a friend than see him ruining himself both financially and physically with the booze.

After swinging from the rafters with Finchy one night at the Carlton Towers Hotel when it was too late to get home, I insisted he pay for my sexual athletics by buying me a present. While he hid under the blankets, I called Dibdin, the Royal Jewelers just down the street, and told them to hack over to the hotel with the best string of pearls they had in the house. If Finchy could spend £500 making strangers happy with free drinks, he could make me happier with a well-earned reward. The man from Dibdin arrived promptly with two blue velvet cases. I let him in and he watched as I struggled with Finchy, trying to get his head out of the bottom of the bed, in which position he'd reversed himself for better cover. The man was fascinated by the bump cowering wrong side up, letting out pain-filled yelps. After I threatened to take both boxes of pearls if Finchy didn't emerge to choose, he allowed his unhappy face to appear and watched me try on the pearls. The real string held a hundred lustrous orbs, but was minute and cost £2,000. The other, more ostentatious rope pleased me better and was cheaper by half, being only "cultured," like the man from Dibdin. Finchy signed the bill, to be directed forthwith to Auntie Ollie, who had a fit. He kept me in bed all day to make love.

Another lost night, we left the Stork Club in the early hours and entered the chauffeur-driven car that was always on call for Finchy. The driver was complaining about the lateness of the hour, and his temper hit fever pitch when we hit a snowstorm half-way home to Mill Hill. Two and a half hours later, we pulled up at the front door of Boundary House. The driver and I congratulated each other. Suddenly we realized that the other passenger was making no attempt to leave the car.

"Come on, Finchy."

"Want old Trev" came from the darkness.

"You what?" I asked him.

"Got to see me old mate."

Trevor Howard lived a little distance away, on a good day a quick mile, but on a night like this with mounds of snow, the idea of trying to reach his house was a laugh. I laughed.

"Drive me to Mr. Howard's house," commanded Finchy in a bad slur.

"Are you out of your mind?"

"You're not well enough, sir, for that long trip," advised the driver.

"Balls, Harry! I want me mate!"

He released a boyishly crooked grin at Harry, which Harry found hard to resist.

"I'll do me best, sir."

"That's the feller."

We set off across the white hills of Herefordshire, inching our way toward poor Trevor's house. As the going got rougher, the atmosphere in the car got tenser. Harry was not pleased, and once again the hell raiser was proving that he beat the world at staying the pace. I dozed off to the sound of Harry's grumbling. Suddenly the car stopped.

"I'm not going another inch!" exploded Harry.

"Oh, come on, matey. It's not as bad as the war."

"I'm not so bloody sure about that, if you want to know."

"Just drive the bleedin' car, mate."

Slowly, Harry adjusted his cap. Dimly I saw him looking through his driver's mirror at Finchy. Finchy stared back under his tortoise lids.

"I've carried you, sir, pissed or sober, far and wide, in the last four years and I've waited for you longer than I've waited for my wife in twenty-five years. I like you Mr. Finch, but I am not going one more inch."

Finchy opened the door of the car.

"All right, mate. We'll walk."

"You crazy bastard! We can't walk in this! We'll be found dead in a ditch. Frozen."

"They say it's warm when you die in the snow. Come on."

Trevor wasn't there to receive his long-lost though unexpected visitor, so after resting for a cigarette on the doorstep, we set off back to Boundary House. I was at death's door for a week, cursing my weakness and him.

14

Tomorrow, and tomorrow, and tomorrow
Creeps in this petty pace from day to day,
To the last syllable of recorded time;
And all our yesterdays have lighted fools
The way to dusty death. Out, out, brief
candle!
Life's but a walking shadow, a poor player
That struts and frets his hour upon the
stage
And then is heard no more.

FINCHY WAS SINKING deeper and deeper into the alcoholic pattern; wild days and nights of drunkenness when he wasn't working and suddenly a dizzying brake on it all and days and nights of darkness and sleep and the lettuce leaf diet as he prepared for the next part. During these periods of convalescence, the house became a morgue, with the children tiptoeing in to look at him in bed, this stranger whom they never really ever saw. I attended him and let him recover, but there was no happiness there. Simply, when he wasn't working or traveling, he was a half-man.

Although making pictures adrenalized him and he could prove to the world that he was an impeccable professional, never being late on the set or even showing signs of a hangover, to the amazement of his playmates from the previous night, his lust to travel followed fast after. Rome, the eternal city, had become our home away from home. Life, therefore, was London life when he worked, parties and clubs and falling into plates of soup and other things. Once, at the home of actor Sir John Mills, Finchy performed the undignified party trick of falling backward into the Millses' roaring fire. They were not amused. Months of discipline on the set during the day, and nights of not knowing whether he was on his ass or on his elbow . . . a wife frustrated and bored and anxious to save or change him . . . and arguments about child things like baptism.

"We should have them done."

"Why?"

"Because it's a blessing."

"Over my dead body." Tilting at windmills again.

"Please. Pretty please?"

"It's bullshit."

"Okay. But one day they're going to ask you why they weren't baptized—like their friends."

"It's a load of old cobblers. I'm not having it."

"Why you so scared of nuns and priests?"

"Don't want to talk about it."

But in Rome he didn't seem frightened of the religious throngs of priests and nuns. Not *en masse,* anyway. He would still touch his privates if a single nun passed him in the street, but he didn't seem to feel such a personal threat in Rome.

"It's different here. It's their place."

Part of the reason Finchy loved Rome was that in Rome nobody treated him like a star. He was among a society of artists and nobody gave a shit that he'd made X number of pounds starring with Susan Hayward, the only actress in the world, they said, who could cry on "Action!"

Nobody expected him to be grand or generous or dress well and they didn't care if he was outrageous. Everyone in Rome was outrageous. He was just another ordinary bloke who'd done well in the moving pics and was a bit of a pisspot, like everyone else. The odd cabdriver would recognize him sometimes and address him as "Dottore," which made him preen his feathers, but Rome was bigger than anyone who visited her.

Bertie Whiting, probably his greatest friend and a spectacularly knowledgeable aficionado of the city, endlessly produced historical anecdotes that enthralled us, although Bertie recalls that after soaking up the secrets of Rome, Finchy never showed his appreciation in kind. He was a mean man in Rome, he was strangely stingy there, unlike in London; in Rome he paid to be poor, like the genuinely penurious painters and writers. At Rosatti's in the Piazza del Popolo, he would spend days and nights among them, drinking *aperitívi* and hearing them gossip about their work, their successes, their broken hearts. There was always someone to talk to and each man bought his own drink. Twenty or thirty of us would sit down to a plate of pasta in the restaurant next door and each pay for himself. Finchy liked that. Sometimes Bertie would lecture him.

"For God's sake, Finchy, be a rich man! I'll give you the name and address of a professional money man in London. Please be a rich man. You can have as much money as you like to spend and *still* be a rich man!"

Finchy would wither him with a terrible look, as if Bertie were about to steal from him.

Nobody in Rome gave it a thought that Finchy was earning immense amounts of money, because he behaved and lived like a poor man, like them. If he had any money in his pockets, you didn't see it.

Bertie, his wife Lorri, a sculptress, and Diana Graves, the marvelously eccentric actress-writer niece of Robert Graves, also experienced the knocking nun as I had. They were driving back from Positano, with Finchy in Bertie's sleek British sports car. One of those mysterious storms that satanically blow up in that part of the world flung itself at the travelers crushed inside the overloaded car. The luggage had been firmly strapped to the roof. Suddenly the travelers were turned to stone. Three loud knocks rapped out on the metal roof of the car. Finchy curled into a petrified ball. "Oh Christ, it's the nun! She's come to get me!" Bertie told him not to be ridiculous and climbed out in the pouring rain to check the straps that held down the suitcases. He thought that one of them might have come loose and was thudding. Soaked and puzzled, he got back into the car to inform the friends that all seemed well up there.

"It's the nun, I tell you."

"What nun, you silly bastard?"

"My nun. She's either after me or trying to warn me!"

Sensitive people, all, they were not about to crush his superstitions or anyone else's. One didn't if one lived in Rome. The Gods were too close. Bertie started up the motor and they continued along the precarious coast road, not at the best of times a route to be taken without due care and attention, because of the twists that wind it close to the cliff wall on one side and a horrendous drop into the ocean on the other.

As Bertie maneuvered another bend in the sleeting downpour, he was horrified to see two huge trucks approaching him, side by side. One truck was overtaking the other. They were all going to be killed! There was no way either truck could alter its position now and nowhere for Bertie to go except to the certain watery grave down below. He galvanized himself while the others whimpered and Finchy concertinaed onto the floor. Had the nun been warning them? Bertie was wondering if there was enough room for the car to pass between the trucks. Through his gritted teeth, he addressed the cringing actor.

"You must tell me about this nun sometime, Finchy."

The trucks seemed to be trying to separate to give space. He'd have to try. Like the demented optimist he was, Bertie drove within a hair's breadth between them. They were safe.

It crossed Bertie's mind that if he hadn't stopped to check the luggage straps, he would have rounded the corner and crashed straight into the one truck as it began to overtake the other; he sternly warned Finchy not to play games again with his sodding nun, if you don't mind! And the party drove back to Rome deeply impressed by their strange experience.

At Tivoli, near Rome, Bertie recited a poem to Finchy. They were going through Hadrian's villa, a mad conglomeration to which the Emperor added buildings he had fancied abroad—a pagoda here, a minaret there, all in all, a sort of architectural history of his battles. The only structure now remaining is the Greek amphitheater. During lunch, Bertie quoted the five-line verse that Hadrian had himself written on his deathbed. Finchy learned the lines quickly and delivered them from the center of the deserted theater:

> Animula vagula, blandula
> Hospes comesque corporis,
> Quae nunc abibis in loca
> Pallidula, rigida, nudula;
> Nec, ut soles, dabis jocos?

Which translates into:

> Little soul, undefined and mild, host and guest of my body,
> What will you do now that you live in a place that is pale,
> Cold and bare—you who were so playful?

While he was there on the stage reciting those lines, a flock of sheep came over to the edge of the arena, flowing like the souls of the dead, listening to his voice.

Years later, because the incident haunted Bertie, he wrote a poem of his own:

> Thick weeds on a bare skyline,
> A fat disgruntled guardian,
> Green lizards flick, the rebuilt
> Pool stares flatly at the brick wall,
> It is all so hot and the thorns crackle.
> But below the hill
> In the overgrown theatre
> As you recited his dying verse,
> Sheep, like souls, flowed in to crop the grass.

Years later, when Finchy began to drink to the point of falling out of his chair, speechless, boring; when he contributed nothing more, had no energy to do so, the artists dropped him. He knew he was rejected, and had the arrogance to blame it on his last wife's black skin. But before the bad end, he could have the best of two worlds in that great city. When the artists left the trattorias to sleep in order to work the following day, he would go off to the Dolce Vita and share the nights with that world. An ideal city for a man who only senses that he feels pain and when he does burrows down into the gutter through the bottom of a bottle.

Solo Syndication and Literary Agency Ltd.

Finchy, 1965.

The flower of Australian manhood.

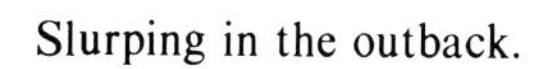

Slurping in the outback.

Solo Syndication and Literary Agency Ltd.

The future looks grim.

"Farming's a serious business, mate."

Finchy in the dreaded gray suit to visit important people.

"Waiting for me mates to git out from that tent."

What he found on the beach. Yolande.

Thanks for the memory.

Honeymoon boat.
"When does this place get there?"

THERE. Hollywood, where there's no THERE—there!

It takes a man
to make a girl.

Solo Syndication and Literary Agency Ltd.

The Japanese bus conductor.

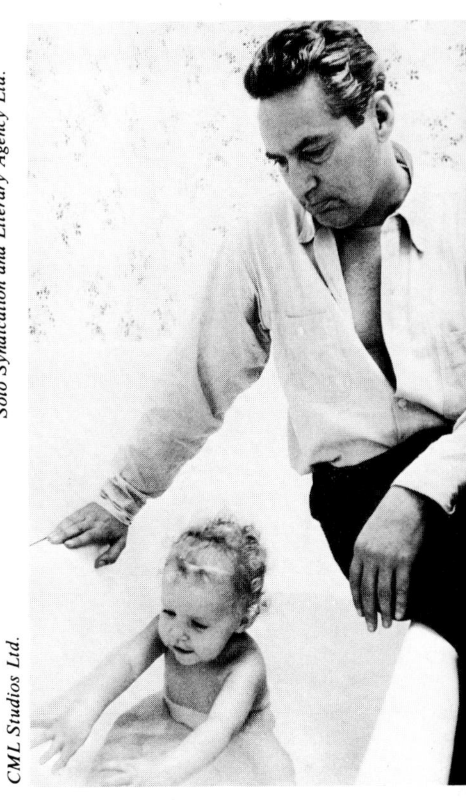

CML Studios Ltd.

The pouting lip that signaled
the wild wet woods.

Solo Syndication and Literary Agency Ltd.

The wild wet woods.

Solo Syndication and Literary Agency Ltd.

"I can't cook either!"

Solo Syndication and Literary Agency Ltd.

Finchy and our Queen.

Wallace Heaton Microlux

Yolande and their Prince—
Bernhard of the Netherlands.

The works.

A ghost of a smile—*Network.*

George Konig

"He told me
many things."

Solo Syndication and Literary Agency Ltd.

The portrait. We're still there.

15

WE WERE FAST spiraling into disaster. Finchy was at the studios all day and I was at home all day or at Lizzie Arden's trying to keep body together. I was told to stop those visits because they were too expensive. I ordered the whole lot down to Boundary House for my treatments. The babies, now four and nearly six, were too young to talk to, but I loved them passionately. When Finchy got home from the bar after filming, they were asleep, and when they woke in the morning, he was gone. I wonder who the hell they thought he was.

I decided to have another dinner party. Being in a state of exquisite boredom by now, I planned these little get-togethers to keep my mind awake. Staying alive. I invited Patrick White, brilliant author of *Voss* and *The Tree of Man,* whom I'd met somewhere; Emlyn Williams, the great actor and playwright of *The Corn Is Green,* and his wife, Molly, an irreverent but highly amusing lady; and *Girl with Green Eyes* Irish author Edna O'Brien and her Hungarian husband, whose name escapes me. Finchy was told to be back from the studios by seven o'clock. I don't think he heard.

Dead on eight, the doorbell rang. Manuelo answered it and ushered in Emlyn and Molly, who both looked extremely relieved to have made it all the way from London.

"It's the end of the world, dear," exclaimed Molly.

"You better believe it," I replied.

Finchy hadn't got back yet.

"Well, dear, we got here and that's wonderful. Where's Peter?"

"He'll be down in a minute." Bastard.

Molly took her martini and stood with her back to the fire, admiring the room. "I feel wonderful," she said. "Nothing, but nothing, could disturb me tonight."

"Let's drink to that," said Emlyn.

"Except for one thing," Molly added.

"What could that be?" I asked.

"Any mention of that cow Edna O'Brien."

Any mention of that cow Edna O'Brien! Christ. That cow was going to walk through the door any minute. I nearly passed out. I heard the doorbell. I was doomed. There was no time to warn Molly, and what good would it do? I looked at Emlyn looking at the pictures. He turned and smiled. If only Finchy were here, but he never was.

O'Brien and spouse entered. Molly turned to stone, Emlyn became a statue and I stood stunned at being guilty of a social gaff that could only end in tears. I heard a car pull up and prayed that it was my drunken spouse. Finchy wandered in and drew up quickly at the sight of Madame Tussaud's in his own drawing room. He glanced at me, finding nothing, hopped over to Molly to lift her frozen body into a bear hug. After putting her down, he turned to Emlyn.

"Emlyn! What a great surprise!"

Emlyn drew himself up. "What do you mean surprise? You knew we were coming a week ago."

"Did I, dear boy?"

"And I wish I hadn't," quipped Emlyn.

Oh God. Molly had turned her back and was glaring into the fireplace. I gave her another martini. She wouldn't look at me, so I couldn't ask what happened to make her hate O'Brien so much. The O'Briens got a gay welcome from Finchy, who moved them into the drinking area. The doorbell screeched.

"Manuelo!" I yelled, quite out of control.

Finchy looked startled. "Calma . . . calma. I'll get it."

I left the room with him, just to get some air. Finchy opened the door and Patrick White stood there, a tall, handsome, somber man.

"Hello," he said politely.

"Hello, mate. And who are you?"

"I am Patrick White."

"Who, mate?"

"Patrick White. And I've been invited to dinner."

"Are you sure, mate?"

"Oh, for God's sake, Peter. This is Patrick White, the great writer. You know he's coming to dinner. Now, shut up and get him in. Oh, excuse me."

Behind Patrick was his companion, a much smaller, pale-faced man, with a briefcase. White introduced him and we all sort of fell into the hall.

Finchy held out his hand to the author. "I'm so sorry, old boy. I'm such a stupid bastard."

Patrick nodded sagely. He introduced his friend.

Back in the chamber of horrors, I found the Hungarian prodding Emlyn in the ribs. Emlyn was backing into a corner parrying the finger with his empty glass. Edna sidled up to Finchy, who introduced her to White. She whispered a compliment and the Australian author accepted it blandly. I dragged him over to Molly. I hardly knew the man, but, from my quickly garbled explanation of the tension in the room, I felt he would be sensitive enough to understand. He seemed to make some sense out of it and started to distract the livid Molly. I hefted more drinks around, stronger than the last lot. How was I going to seat them? Out of the back of my head, I heard the Hungarian say to Emlyn, "I never thought much of you as an actor, anyway."

Emlyn became apoplectic. "How dare you talk to me like that? How dare you even talk to me, you Middle European turd?"

"Don't even talk to him, Emlyn." Molly swayed and Patrick White took her arm.

Edna, with the aplomb that comes from years of criticism and catechism, sipped at her glass. Finchy was beginning to look as though he had forgotten the lines to the drama.

"Dinner is ready, madame."

"Oh, thank God. I mean, good!"

Molly shot me a terrible look. I took her arm and firmly guided her into the dining room.

"Sit there," I ordered.

The table was oblong. It was going to be difficult to separate the gladiators. It would have been difficult if the table had been horseshoe.

"I'll sit at the head. Then I can see you all," Finchy said, sitting down next to Molly, and I quickly seated White's companion next to her and Edna on the same side, next to him so that the women had a human barrier between them. Emlyn sat opposite his wife, I grabbed the chair in the center, separating him from the Hungarian, and White took the other head. Dinner commenced.

"So you write, do you?" asked Finchy pleasantly.

"I have that neurotic compulsion, yes," replied White.

"You sly bitch." There was no mistaking whom Molly was addressing.

"What do you mean?" The Irish slur, from Edna.

"You know perfectly well what I mean."

"Well, I don't."

"Slut."

"Don't take your racial prejudice out on me."

"Racial prejudice? What racial prejudice?"

"I thought you were Irish, too, Molly, like Emlyn," remarked Finchy, pouring the vino around.

Suddenly I was quite out of the picture. I didn't know there was racial disharmony between the Welsh and the Irish. They're all Celts.

"You put your name on that crit in *Harper's* and you didn't write it! And don't say you did."

Emlyn had just written a book on the Moor murders, a ghastly history of child sex and murder that had horrified Britain, which loves to be horrified by its morbid, sexually devious crimes.

"I know your husband wrote it. Even you couldn't have regurgitated such junk! And it was a great book!"

I noticed Patrick White sliding his chair back for a better view. He knew good material when he saw it. Finchy's glass stopped at his lips. A rare occurrence. Emlyn got to his feet.

"To have come all this way and to have to sit at the same table as you two mediocrities—one who can't even speak the King's English and has the audacity to review *my* book! I have never been so insulted in all my life. Appalled!"

Molly was on her feet now. Edna and her husband stood up; the cat jumped onto White's lap and he stroked it; Finchy's eyes widened and my hands shook as I whipped the banana flambé around in a scorched pan.

"Never again will we go out of London. It's been the most ghastly experience of our lives!"

Suddenly the room was empty. I heard the cars going. Patrick slowly got to his feet and took my hands.

"Brilliant, my dear. Quite brilliant."

I was flattered but confused.

Then he, too, departed.

At last Finchy and I were alone. We sat at the table and had another bottle of wine together.

"Well, that one will go down for posterity."

"I didn't know. I really didn't."

"Let's go to bed and I'll do a painting for you."

I didn't know whether to groan or take him in my arms. Upstairs, I watched him paint a dynamic landscape on a piece of wallpaper, using the kitchen ingredients he kept in the bathroom. I quite loved him then, because he didn't reprimand me for being so dumb or trying too hard. We fell asleep in each other's arms.

The first person to call the following morning was Patrick White.

"I want to compliment you," he said. "It takes genius to put together a table of natural enemies. I hope you don't mind if I use the story in one of my books one day."

Later on, somebody told me Molly wrote a short story about the evening and I'm recounting it now, so I suppose one can always wet a parched tongue on a sour grape.

There were other parties that were immensely more successful than that particular effort. I remember when Dirk Bogarde rang Finchy to ask him, at her specific request, to Judy Garland's birthday. Usually, never a man to be flattered, Finchy was more pleased that Dirk, an actor Finchy hugely admired, had bothered to call him.

Dirk had a beautiful country mansion and was a superb host. He had gathered some eighty heavyweights for the party. Finchy was on his best behavior and I was thrilled.

Noel Coward sat down at the piano and called Judy to sit beside him.

"I've written a little piece. I'll play it for you."

He started to play and sing the songs from his new musical, *Sailors Away*.

"I love it," said Judy.

"I want you to have it as a birthday present. I know you'll never play in it, but it's yours."

Judy wept with happiness and so did many of the rest of us. Then the two magical people sang many songs together, taking us to a room with a view somewhere over the rainbow.

At last *The Seagull* with Vanessa Redgrave was set to go. Finchy, in his profoundly secretive way, was burrowing into Chekhov, accumulating a certain morosity in his behavior that apparently becomes the poor Russian playwright. Everyone in England seemed to interpret Chekhov with a certain deadly heaviness, which usually put a quite unnecessary burden on the works, and it looked as though Finchy was going to fall into the trap.

But Finchy and I, despite the occasional good times, were wearing one another down. And inevitably, the time came we both agreed that I had to get away from him—for both our sakes. Finchy took us to the airport and waved us good-bye. We neither of us felt happy and clung together when the time came. We'd been married for six years now and some of it had been so very good. I wondered what was going to become of us all. I had, of course, thought of divorce, but divorce, after resisting marriage, seemed a cowardly end to love. With these melancholy thoughts in mind, I left England for an Italian holiday without Finchy.

Amy Kelly, our Jamaican mammy, came along to cope with Charles, who had not changed since birth. Did I need her! The four of us sat on the beach and watched the dark Italians playing and eating ice cream. Sea and sand soothe me, so I soon began to feel younger or less drugged by anguish. And as I looked around me, life did look as though it could be good and even happy, though I wouldn't have bet on it. We started to relax, frequently taking a little boat among the coves and swimming and sleeping in the sun. Perhaps there was a chance Finchy and I could patch it up.

A few weeks after we'd arrived, the doorbell rang. I answered it to an unfamiliar young man.

"Are you Yolande Finch?"

"Yes. Why?" I felt like having company and he looked so pleasant.

"I'm from the———. Have you any comment to make on the affair your husband's having with Shirley Bassey?"

I could see it all in long shot. I stood there dumbfounded. What did people say in situations like this? I tried to remember. Something about "no comment"?

"No comment?"

"So you know about it then?"

"No comment."

"Can we have some pictures."

"No thank you."

"Of you and the children?"

"No."

"I'll wait downstairs."

"Don't bother."

I closed the door. Wait downstairs! We wouldn't be able to go to the beach. What affair? Why hadn't Finchy told me? Shirley Bassey! What was he doing?

From then on we were invaded by the press. It amazed me that they would bother to send reporters so long a way for a story.

"Did you know Finchy's being cited by Bassey's husband?"

"No comment."

"It's been announced that you and Finchy are separated."

"No comment."

"Did you know that Finchy's publicist, Rex Berry, says you and Finchy have parted?"

I didn't even know Finchy had a publicist.

"Are you going to divorce Mr. Finch and cite Shirley Bassey?"

"No comment."

"Has Finchy told you he loves Shirley?"

"No comment. Please."

We had returned to London, where there were meetings with Tony Richardson and the cast and the seriousness of the whole affair seemed to depress or just terrify Finchy. He became withdrawn and moody, drinking steadily, but there were no jokes or twinkling anymore. I was dreading *The Seagull,* because I knew what it was like for one in a marriage to be working in the West End while the other waits at home.

Floundering on, I gave another lunch at the house. One of the guests was a very famous critic's wife, estranged from him by mutual consent. He had thrown her out after finding her naked in the elevator with a man. A heavy tippler herself, I suppose I invited her because she was clever and I wanted to distract Finchy, as well as myself. There were three others to lunch, but the sequence of events that day quite blots their identities from my memory.

At four o'clock the luncheon was still going strong. Gallons of wine had been put away and I realized it was still far from over. Some people never know when to go home. Of course the lady didn't have one anymore, so there was no rush for her. At last the other guests departed and the three of us launched into the late afternoon drinking, the drinking in the sunlight that I always find particularly depressing. Finchy clowned and told stories all afternoon and I must say that for a small woman, she held her drink like a stoker. I left to be sick around seven. When I got back, they'd started another bottle. I suggested dinner at the local Chinese restaurant, thinking that could be the first step to getting her out of the house. Two hours later, we were back, drunker.

The night closed in. I knew she had no car—and suggested calling her a taxi. I don't think they even heard me. I went upstairs, trying very hard to forget "the night of the Gay Divorcée," knowing well that the way things were going, the lady was going to jump Finchy sooner or later. As I locked my door, my feeling was that if they wanted to make it together, at least I'd let them do it out of my sight and get it over with.

Some time later, I heard Finchy coming up the stairs calling my name. He tried the door and, finding it locked, started beating on it and yelling to let him in. I let him in and started back to bed.

"Has she gone?"

"Fucking women. You're all the same!"

He was very drunk and suddenly looked like a small, dangerous bull. I wondered what had disturbed him. I sensed that he hated himself very much more then than I did.

"What do you mean?"

"You're all fucking whores!"

I hit him. For the first time in our life together, I struck him. I was disgusted with myself because we were not battering people. He stood there tight and angry for a second and then incredibly let fly with his fist. The anger erupted and I sprang at him and we fought across the room. As we struggled and pushed, slugging with open hands so as not to hurt too much, I felt more anguish than terror and saw the tears in his eyes. At last, we sat beside each other at the bottom of the bed, our heads lowered onto our arms.

I left our room and slowly descended the stairs. I knew she would still be there and she was, lying half naked across the sofa, part of her underwear on the carpet. I stared at her, thinking of the children seeing this and wondering how women could be such pigs. I called a hire car, woke her and told her to get dressed. Neither of us spoke as she left. Checking that the children were still in dreamland, I went back to Finchy. He lay on the bed staring at the ceiling and quietly I got under the sheets and turned my back on him, carefully, not wanting to show him that he had had his last chance.

Finchy enclosed himself in his role in *The Seagull* and I decided I would soon return to Italy to soak out some of my isolation and bitterness in the sun.

16

I HAD STAYED in London for the opening night of *The Seagull*, which was received with reverence by the critics. Vanessa and Finchy alike received accolades, not that either of them showed much enthusiasm for the praise. I thought Finchy's performance was cold and remote, and Vanessa's misty heroine dangerously close to one of Dracula's passive naifs. They did make a pair. Again, I was forced to wonder why Chekhov had to be played so bloody bloodlessly. The only actress who seemed to understand that tragedy inevitably mixes with wit was Peggy Ashcroft, and the line delivered by Anne Beach as Masha, "I'm in mourning for my life," quite enthralled me, hitting the nail on the head about mine.

I saw the play a couple of times but preferred to go round the corner to watch Peter O'Toole doing *Hamlet* and giving a quite extraordinary performance. He had spiced up the poor Danish Prince and put in one or two little gags of his own. Sir Michael Redgrave was most unhappy that, night after night, at the conclusion of the gravedigger's scene, O'Toole would turn toward the court, trooping on the funeral of Ophelia, led by Redgrave, who played the wicked stepfather, and announce, "Here comes the King, the queen!—and all the courtiers," when the line should have gone, "And here comes the King, the Queen, the courtiers."

Mostly, however, I stayed at Boundary House and climbed the

walls. Knowing he was in bad odor at home, Finchy naturally sank into his old habits and fell in at five o'clock each morning. I pretended not to give a damn. In fact I pretended so well that Frank Sinatra had commented on it. I had gone to a charity concert Frankie gave for some royal cause attended by the Queen and Prince Philip and had the fortune or misfortune to be placed in the front row, center. I worship Sinatra and his singing that night was sublime. I was sure that I was no cool audience, because, if anything, I overreact when moved, and he moves me. Therefore, I was dumbfounded when later, at the supper given for him and on being introduced to him, he said, "Give a damn!"

"What, Mr. Sinatra?"

"You sat there all night looking like plastic."

"That's impossible!" I protested. "I think you're the greatest thing since the Old Testament!"

"Well, you didn't look like it. So, do yourself a favor. Give a damn."

I must have been losing the light in my eyes for some time for him to have seen it from the stage!

There didn't seem much point in my holding old Boundary House together up in Mill Hill. By now the "wild wetters" were the order of the day. I didn't ask him anymore where they were, but to judge from his face, they weren't getting him on the road to contentment. He would turn in at dawn to sleep for the day and take off at about six for the West End. One day Samantha asked who he was, so I decided he wouldn't miss us if we returned to Italy for a few weeks. If, as he had often said, one could never "unlove" someone, I, anyway, had come to a state of unfeeling. We were both perplexed. It was sad, and I told him so.

He stared into his glass. He took another drink and so did I. I heard the sea lapping below and the sounds of voices and Vespa motors drifted up. I bet he's going to get somberly plastered, I thought, and I'll stay calm for a bit and get drunk, too.

"Please talk to me."

"Nothing to say."

"We have to be able to talk."

He glanced at me, his eyes distant and dark.

"Please."

"Leave me alone, Yo. It's something I have to get out of my system."

"You mean you love Shirley? What's love?"

"No. Leave it."

"I can't."

I wondered how it would end. All the traumas blocked and closed inside. All those years of loneliness and suffering cemented and packed away. He couldn't trust me, because he had nothing to trust with. I'd never be able to crack that shell, never.

The hours slipped by as together we sat there, watching the sun sink, drinking and hoping, praying that some *deus ex machina* would break the knotted silence. I tried to talk, but I was lost, too. How I wished I was sixty years old and could have taken him in my arms and comforted him and felt no jealousy. But I was too young for this man's pain and too young for ours and too young altogether for this scene . . . this non-scene. The more I insisted on his attention, on an explanation, the colder he became. All I wanted was the truth, I told him, knowing that there is no truth about things like that. If I'd been his friend, or a man, I would have battened down the hatches and kept peace.

"Just leave me. Just leave me alone."

I cried a little and kept up with him drink for drink.

"Let's go and have something to eat."

We joined some people I'd met at the local trattoria. I suddenly felt amazingly gay and proud of my famous husband because everyone deferred to him and treated him like a king. Finchy remained somber and aloof, which further impressed the fashionable group, and I, hating him, was pleased that once upon a time he had been mine. Suddenly I decided to leave. He didn't follow me. I got in the car and drove to a young man's boat and sat with him in the dark, telling him my maudlin story. We kept drinking and he tried to take me to bed, imagining that tenderness might heal the wounding, but I couldn't make it. At last I left. Drunkenly, I drove the car back to the apartment and crashed it neatly into the wall of the building. Finchy was lying on the couch in the sitting room as I passed through into the bedroom. We looked at each other speechlessly. The words of Scarlett O'Hara kept going through my mind, "Tomorrow is another day." I felt that if I could just sleep enough, everything would be all right—yes—everything would be all right tomorrow, "because tomorrow is another day." I threw down a couple of barbiturates. During what was left of the night, I threw down a couple more. I kept thinking I must sleep, but I couldn't or it felt as though I was not sleeping when probably I was. If I could just sleep, tomorrow we could talk and be sensible and work things out. It wasn't the end of the world! I never woke up.

The doctor told Finchy that it was too late for a stomach pump because the drugs had gone into the bloodstream. Finchy agreed to an insulin injection in the heart. "We can only give her three," said the doctor.

I was unconscious for two days. The third shot brought me back to life.

As I woke I saw the nun's face over me and the wooden cross on the white wall. Finchy was lying across the room on a narrow bed in the fetal position. I wondered if he was dead, too. The nun smiled at me and took my hand.

17

"ONCE YOU GET into the hands of lawyers, mate, we've had it."

And so say all of us.

Finchy didn't want a divorce. The very idea made him pale. We stumbled around a few platitudes. When, recovered, I got back to the apartment after the suicide bit, he was incredibly sweet and loving with me and the children, but it was over and we both knew it. We stayed together for a few days before he had to get back to London and *The Seagull.* When he left, I took him to the train and told him I'd be home soon and I'd seek a divorce.

"Don't do it, luv. I don't want a divorce."

I was frightened, too. I'd never had a divorce. I didn't even know where or how one found a lawyer.

"But, darling, it's not over with Shirley, is it?"

"I can't talk about it. Just let me work it out."

"Can't."

I knew the affair wasn't over and whichever way I looked at it, even if it was, there'd be another sometime and maybe another, and then I'd start cheating, and we'd end up with one of those marriages in name only. I couldn't face it and I didn't want it. Marriage to old Finchy made me tired. I wanted out. I knew my brush with death hadn't been entirely an accident. I wanted to live, even if I couldn't be happy, but living with this man would bring me to the edge again, or worse, I might just be tempted to push him, when he was standing too close to the edge of something. Murder! Either way, who'd bring up the children? Ma? It struck me as droll that Finchy, the partner with the creative death syndrome, might be the one to come out of it all unscathed.

He wasn't at Boundary House when we got back, but he called to say he was staying away for a few days to work things out. On my part, I started to look around for the elusive "attorney with muscle," something I'd read about in a Hollywood movie rag.

I called my ex-agent, Laurence Evans, who'd cared about me once upon a time, and asked for an interview with him, explaining the problem. Smug as a Muggeridge, he invited me over to his flat in Eaton Square.

His wife received me at the door in fluffy bedroom booties which fascinated me as I followed her through to the great presence. Larry allowed himself a knowing smile, followed immediately with his "concerned" look.

"I told you you shouldn't have married him."

"Yeah, well I did. And I want a lawyer. How do I find one?"

"He's got no money, Yo. You mustn't expect to get much."

"Well, he must have some. He's been working ever since I met him."

"Well."

"Well, where is it? You all get your ten percent. There must be a little left for us. No?"

"I doubt it, Yo."

He rubbed his hands together. Was Larry going to make it even harder for me, I wondered.

We had tea and he gave me the name of a man, who, he explained, was brilliant at making money for himself. Maybe he would give me a hand. He sincerely hoped so, he said, as he got to his feet. I sincerely thanked him for giving me his time and his wife appeared again to take me to the door. Our parting was so sincere, I couldn't help but feel I'd been given the brush off. I could see that to an agent I was the expendable one in this affair.

I went back to Boundary House and picked some roses. Parting the hedge that gave our house privacy from the road, I remembered some of the fun times. Just so recently, a few years ago, there had been that face peering through just those leaves—Evans, Finchy's private M.I.5 trouble-shooter. Banned from Finchy's presence, the dick had started to hang around my hedge. I told him he'd read too many *Photoplay* magazines and to please go back to his fiancée.

God, I missed the fool. Full of doubts and love and nostalgia, I went through Finchy's clothes and books and paintings. All the *memento mori* of a man well worth loving for a woman who had the skin of a rhino and could swing from the trees.

He looked terribly small in the stills I had of him. When Irving Allen, the producer of *Oscar Wilde,* first considered Finchy for the part, he decided, "Much too short." But then, Irving had a thing that actors should be tall. He thought Finchy would be a great actor if he'd wear lifts. *Everybody* would have to wear lifts. Emrys Jones, a lovely Welsh actor was up to play Wilde's best friend, and Emrys was rather tiny. Jimmy Ligatt, casting, told Emrys to get the tallest lifts he could find. Emrys came to the interview like Fonteyn on points; his lifts were practically surgical boots. Irving Allan received him from behind his desk as Emrys torturously gave the producer a rundown on his theatrical career. At last it was agreed that he play the part and he tottered out of the office. When he'd gone, Irving told Jimmy, "He'll have to wear lifts and he'll be just fine." Irving had such a thing about heights, he made *The Towering Inferno.*

Shirley Bassey, the Tigress from Tiger Bay, Cardiff, was divorced by her husband, Kenneth Hume, that year, sixty-five. She was accused of adultery and Finchy was named corespondent. Hume also claimed that the child born to her in sixty-three was not his and blood tests supported his suspicions. When Finchy called, pissed, at four o'clock one morning to tell me he loved me, I asked him if they'd been having an affair for years and years without my knowing. He told me not to be an asshole and that the only reason he'd started the bloody thing was because I'd deserted him and gone to Italy. I'd often wondered how many little Finchys there were populating the world.

Finchy announced that he wasn't going to marry Shirley Bassey. Perhaps by my reading that in the press he thought I would be reassured that he didn't love her. I think I knew that already.

To me it seemed as if he had meant it when he said he didn't want a divorce. He was calling almost every night now. But maddeningly, his calls were always too late at night or at dawn, when the truth was coming to him from the bottom of the bottle. I didn't want him to tell me anything drunk. I wanted it straight out sober. Weeks went by while we stuck to our absurd poses. On reflection, I think he played it straighter than I did. I wanted him to take me out to dinner, by candlelight, and woo me back. He thought I should take him back the way he was and always had been. I wanted him to come and sleep on the mat outside the door again and he wanted just to come back and move in. No games. He was honest and I wanted him to pay. We were stuck.

I had seen the self-made millionaire lawyer whom Laurence Evans had suggested so sincerely. He told me that I should be satisfied to receive about a thousand pounds a year and be grateful for it.

"But there must be more money than that!"

"I doubt it."

"Where is it then? Disappeared into some Gruyère cheese?"

He laughed merrily, his disinterest apparent. I didn't like him very much, so I didn't cry, which usually brings out the best in men like that. I'd have need of those tears, anyway, and didn't feel I should waste them on another male chauvinist, like my beloved or Larry Evans.

Within the next two years I went through three more lawyers until Robin Douglas Hume put me onto the real expert, Derek Clogg, of Theodore Goddard, who did everybody's divorce and always won for the lady in distress. By this time, I was fed up, having been on the receiving end of Finchy's adviser's little punishments. Nasty. The invisible team had started to put the squeeze on and I didn't like it. I got the impression that if I stopped being a silly girl and stopped wanting to divorce Finchy, everything could be all right again.

My allowance was cut off and all my credit accounts at the stores curtailed. I was livid. Unbelievably, the heating was turned off at home. "We've been instructed not to deliver more coal, madame." Mr. Maskell, the gardener, got the boot, and the tomatoes began to wither. I went down with the children to look at the chickens pecking each other to death. I never went back and let somebody come and take them away. The garden was a shambles, weeds celebrating in a violent crusade against the neat lawns and dainty flowers. The swing sofa that had rocked us on warm and happier days looked like a decrepit invention half finished, and the Spanish couple wept as they abandoned us. I'd let Amy Kelly go, after she'd set fire to the ironing board, let the bath overflow and left open the little gate at the top of the stairs, tempting the intrepid Charles to walk down them at a pace that cracked his collarbone. Chaos, dreaded chaos, was approaching fast.

The children and I huddled upstairs, a feeling of doom pervading the pretty house. It was winter. I was lonely and I was frightened.

Apparently, the affair with Shirley was losing its momentum. Rumor had it that Finchy was getting restless under certain pressures laid on him by relatives of his mistress. Finchy was often found topping up at the bar at Gerry's, complaining into his cups that "they're crucifying me, mate!" Most of London assumed it was I who was crucifying him and that made me even more touchy and neurotic. What with practically all services cut from Boundary House, I was beginning to think Finchy was being vindictive in the extreme or allowing himself to be bullied into subduing and torturing me by Cosa Nostra methods. If they really wanted us out of the house, the next menace could be a firebomb in the baybushes outside the front door. That didn't seem like Finchy, but remembering his remark about lawyers, certain suspicions haunted my already wobbly sense of security.

Because Finchy was never one for "possessions," I felt pretty sure he wouldn't send in the mob to dismantle the house. After all, Finchy was dedicated to the line from *It Happened One Night,* which had impressed him as a teenager, when Clark Gable, driving along in a car with Claudette Colbert, says, "I don't want to own anything that doesn't go in a suitcase."

Taking him at his word, I gathered together his second pair of jeans, his black silk socks—seven and a half pairs—and the rest of his miserable wardrobe. I took all his bloody awards and wrapped them in a curtain and stuffed them in a box. I didn't want them, for sure.

I needed to resume my career and I knew that I'd have to scratch my way back into the profession. I asked a photographer to photograph me for *Spotlight,* the actors' reference book. I'd always had a quarter page, a position I didn't deserve and couldn't afford. Perhaps someone would recognize the fighting spirit and reward me with a lead, a common delusion, I was prepared to try. What I needed was personal contact.

I went to see one of the directors of *Spotlight* who since the very beginning of my career in London had told me I should establish myself through the repertory companies. He'd always been right, of course, but I'd never agreed with him, my nature demanding the quickest method with the least effort. Pushing regrets aside, I asked his advice once more.

"You'll have to start all over again and join a rep."

"Where?"

"Perhaps Llandudno or Pitlochrie?"

"You've got to be kidding."

"It'll show them you really are serious."

"I am really serious."

"Well, there you go, then."

"Just bye the bye, what should I do with the children? Do you suggest?"

"There must be somewhere you can leave them, dear."

I felt like strangling him. "We don't have communal crèche's *yet*, y'know."

"We all have to sacrifice something for our art, dear."

"Peter doesn't."

"But he's a great actor, dear."

"There is sacrifice and sacrifice," I replied tartly. "Children, I feel, should not be."

"You're very talented, dear, but you'll never make it that way."

I felt like the actor who had played his heart out in some rotten piece in New York watched by many friends. Afterward, no one wanted to tell him how bad he'd been. Noel Coward, a supremely kind man, made the remark that said it all when he entered the dressing room.

" 'Good,' my dear," he said, taking the actor's hands, "is not the word for it."

More exquisite than being damned with faint praise.

So, whatever else was crumbling, it seemed that to survive in the big top, I'd have to play the same game with our children that had been played on Finchy as a child. Neon lights were advertising "Selfishness Wins." I thought about it for a couple of seconds and junked it.

The three of us moved into my bedroom and cozily snuggled up in my seven-by-seven marriage bed at night, a roaring fire in the grate. I felt a tremendous loving and protection toward Samantha and Charles and whatever happened, I decided, we were not going to end up in a one-room flat in Nottinghill Gate.

Suddenly one night, the lights went off. It's always amazed me, and still does, that when light goes, a sort of paralysis steps in. After the first shock of the dark, the fire seemed to brighten and I went in search of the candles I knew I'd seen just a few days, a few weeks, months before. My gall rose as I hunted with the only flashlight in the house. How many hundreds of flashlights had we bought that were not there now. Fuck you, Finch, I swore silently. Fuck you. I'm going to fight!

I pointed the strong headlights of the Mercedes at the front door, bundled the children into the back seat, locked the doors of Boundary House and drove into London and straight to the Hyde Park Hotel. I couldn't believe that Finchy, one of nature's gentlemen, so utterly polite to everyone, even the most atrocious of company, the man who couldn't tolerate violence, the man who wept for the poor, the gentleman, could be doing these vicious things. I'd dismissed him as the perpetrator of the punitive series of incidents and didn't have to look far to find the culprit. He was weak, yes, but a monster, most certainly not. I'd have to see him and talk. Things couldn't end this way.

The Hyde Park Hotel was surprised, but welcoming. They gave us a nice suite overlooking the park. I didn't ask the price. I was going to remain in residence until everybody stopped being vindictive. Was I being vindictive? Why couldn't I take a little infidelity that only half the world knew about by now. Was I gutless or bourgeoise? I hated myself.

We ordered three sole *meunières* for dinner and a special side dish of creamed spinach, which was my favorite. The Hyde Park was much nicer than home anyway. Tomorrow the lawyers could talk.

It took me nearly two years to get the divorce. Lawyers love that. My defiant spree at the Hyde Park brought quick action. They told me to look for a suitable flat. I found one in Knightsbridge belonging to a princess.

Finchy kept working and nobody would touch me with a dead policeman. He made a picture with Sophia Loren called *Judith*, which shall be nameless in Jerusalem. *Far from the Madding Crowd,* with Julie Christie, *A Bequest to the Nation* with Glenda Jackson, a thing in Iceland with huskies, I suppose, and God knows how many others. Auntie Ollie was keeping him busy. I never saw him around London and heard from Bertie that when he wasn't slaving, he spent his time in Rome. He didn't call anymore.

I froze his assets when my lawyers discovered he was planning to transfer everything to the Bahamas. I was surprised that Finchy was overnight becoming a businessman trying to protect his money. The press covered my move in the High Court. I became archvillainess!

At last the day arrived for the final hearing. Dressed in black, like Mary, Queen of Scots, I arrived, looking heartbroken. I'd been told to. Actually, I was feeling the way I always felt ten minutes before curtain call. Sick.

The Temple off the Strand glittered ominously under the winter sun. Sneakily, I wondered if he'd managed to escape to the "wild wet woods" in Nassau with all the money in a suitcase. Images of his stuffing seventy thousand pounds into a suitcase made me smile.

I hurried along the dreary corridors within the building, with my four advisers. Finchy strolled toward us from the opposite direction, also accompanied by members of the law. He gave me a crooked smile and we entered the private chamber. We both felt ridiculous, I'm sure, but I couldn't help thinking, This is all so terribly filmic, and wished someone would call cut, so that we, the main actors, could settle down to discuss the real motives behind the plot. It was not to be. Destiny, set in motion, rolled forward.

The solid twelve-foot table stood aggressively in the center of the room, encircled by its empty chairs. Like members of a wake, my side gravitated solemnly to the window side, putting our backs to the light. Finchy's entourage flapped and settled opposite us. We were twelve in all. Finchy sat directly facing me. What a way to end a love affair, I thought. His expression was mild, perhaps a little amused at all the theatricality. We both had Queen's councils, and as they got to their feet, so did we. I thought we might be about to say grace. The Registrar had arrived and took his place at the head of the table.

I felt Finchy's foot under the table and moved mine closer to him.

> From year to year, the battles, sieges, fortunes
> That I have pass'd;
> I ran it through, even from my boyish days . . .
> And often did beguile her of her tears
> When I did speak of some distressful stroke
> That my youth suffer'd.

> My story being done,
> She gave me for my pains a world of sighs.
> She swore, in faith, 'twas strange, 'twas passing strange . . .
> She loved me for the dangers I had pass'd,
> And I lov'd her that she did pity them.

Yes, my Othello . . . all that.

The voices around us argued and fought. We sat like children at a grown-up's party. Would it never end? "Once we're in the hands of lawyers, mate, we've had it." If I won, I'd give him back the money and we'd catch a banana boat to Jamaica.

I won.

We rose from the battlefield, our eyes holding. Finchy shrugged his shoulders and opened his hands in that Italian gesture that signifies nothing.

"Good-bye?" he said.

"Good-bye."

Finchy walked out of the room and took the next flight to Nassau.

18

WHEN FINCHY FLEW out from England that same September day in 1968, he was to disappear for two years. But I knew where he was. He was playing the Abo at Bamboo, our piece of land in Jamaica. I wondered if he was sleeping under the trees or if he had bought a tent. At least he'd made it back to the land to dig and plant and prune the trees we'd planted. There was a toothless old Jamaican fellow there who kept a couple of chickens and squatted. I hoped they'd find lots to talk about.

The nearest village was at least three miles. He'd be walking everywhere. I could picture him shirtless and barefoot, walking down the dusty tracks to get food and tobacco and perhaps a drink at some native bar.

He'd dropped out, fired his dear Auntie Ollie, and was nowhere to be found in a picture. Gone to earth. People asked where he was. Once, I thought of flying to him, but only once. I knew that one day he'd come out of it. Whatever playing the farmer gave him, the need he had to possess soil and land and earth and to try to produce things from it possessed him. He had to face his fierce aloneness, like a man who spends his life on a long search but doesn't know where the call comes from. He doesn't know what the answers are, or even worse, what the questions are. Like Kipling's cat, "all places were alike to him," probably because if he was ever to identify with that distant voice, it wouldn't matter where he was; he was still an actor through and through. A mummer. Endearingly attached to his art, before a performance, he'd say, "Well, I must go and depict now." He'd always be an actor and he knew that no plantation would keep him from it. I knew that, too, always.

In London I was still knocking on doors and occasionally I'd get something. Financially, at least, we had our three little bums in the honey. The courts had been kind, swatting him for a little extra because he liked nightclubs and didn't like baptisms. Although, or perhaps, because I was well provided for, it wasn't easy getting a job. It seemed I'd bucked the system. Lots of ladies married to actors had taken a lot more shit than I and they were still there keeping the home fires burning and giving interviews about their glorious husbands who could do no wrong, when everyone knew those same men were screwing the ass off anything in skirts.

Once again, Finchy rose like the phoenix from the ashes. He found someone to love, Aletha Barrett, a Jamaican girl with a small boy-child. Perhaps he sometimes thought of his Charles. They became lovers and she gave him a daughter.

People said that he'd changed. The face looked haunted, perhaps a little bitter, and he wasn't a fun drunk anymore. He pushed Roderick Mann, our best British show-business columnist and longtime friend and defender, out of a taxi in Rome because Roddy disagreed with him over something. A man who, if anything, had erred on the side of forgiveness, Roddy was deeply hurt by the incident.

Finchy's health was beginning to decline, too. Insurers wouldn't cover him on his pictures and the film companies had to take the chance he'd make it through to the last day. It was his heart.

By now I'd taken a lease on a little villa in Kensington. The newspaper lady on the corner of Gloucester Road told me she had seen Finchy often. I tried to track him down and came up against an immovable object, Aletha. She told me to leave her man alone.

"I only want him to see his children, Mrs. Finch," I explained plaintively.

"You just want his money," she replied.

They sold Bamboo and bought a banana plantation. Naturally.

In all those years, I only saw him once, as he was lunching alone at the Caprice. He looked handsome, but lonely. I was with another woman and I asked the waiter to tell Mr. Finch that his last wife would like him to come over. We kissed each other.

"I'm over from Jamaica to talk about a film," he said.

"Please come and see the children."

"Righto."

"When?"

"Today?"

"I'll expect you at five. Here's the address."

He arrived dead on time. Samantha and Charles were dressed and waiting and I was timorously excited. When the doorbell rang we all ran to open it. He stood there with a wicker basket filled with Guinness stout.

"It's all they'll let me have," he explained as he put it down. There must have been twenty bottles.

He kissed the children, keeping an eye on me.

"I thought we'd go for a walk," I said.

"Come on, Daddy," said Charles, taking his hand. "We'll show you the round pond."

Finchy looked down at his son. "What's it like to be so small?"

"Well," said Charles, "it's good for hiding, but it's not so good when you want to find something."

Samantha twisted round slowly, her little face filled with loving. We walked slowly to the pond.

"I don't like England now," Finchy said. "It makes me feel old."

"It makes me feel safe."

"Yes. But you'd never let your boat leave the harbor, would you?"

"Where are you living now?"

"We've got a place with the bloody Swiss."

He didn't want to talk about Jamaica.

"Why don't you live in Rome? You love Rome."

"Well, you should live in Rome. Take the children to Rome."

"What would I do in Rome?"

"Be happy."

"Are you?"

"What?"

"Happy?"

And he was quiet.

Back at Launceston Place, he opened his first bottle of stout. I helped him drink it, splicing mine behind a cabinet with bubbly. I didn't want to show him any extravagance, because he'd always thought my taste for champagne unnecessary and I'd always felt champagne should be for the people because its such a silly drink and makes you feel gay. The babies, to me, always babies, although now both older than six, went upstairs. The surprise of him was over for them. He was real, he existed, they'd seen him and now he'd probably stay.

Finchy took me in his arms. I lay there inside them, a little stiff with fright, wanting to want him. We stood up against each other, pressing a little. He smelt of Guinness and I longed to be able to kiss the odor away: to suck him clean of everything, to make him new and lick him and warm him. He started to pull me toward the stairs. I hung back and he pulled harder. As old as time, the instinct that makes women different from men warned my well-tuned sexual senses that if we made love then, one of us would be satisfied completely and one of us would be satisfied locally. If we made love now, it would be Finchy who would enjoy the full reward. I knew that afterward I would be staring at the ceiling feeling a little less again.

"I can't make love to you, Finchy. I want you to love the children."

He started putting all his bottles back in the basket.

"Well, luv. I'm off then."

"Can't you love the fucking children, you cunt?" I screamed. "They need you now!"

"Sorry, luv. That's something else."

"If only, Finchy, you could have kept your prick in perspective, we may have been able to survive."

That was the last time we saw him, although he came looking for us. When he did, though, none of us was there.

19

A VOODOO SPELL was going to be the cause of Peter Finch's death, or so Finchy believed two years before he died.

It was 1974 that he made his last visit to the house in Launceston Place, where the children and I were still living. He arrived sometime after eight in the evening. Tilly, my black South African helper, heard the doorbell ring. She went to the door and looked through the peephole. Recognizing him immediately, although she had seen him only in stills, she opened the door, still keeping it on the chain. He must have been surprised to see Tilly's dark, bright face.

"I want to see my family," he said.

"Please come in, Master Finch."

Finchy followed her through to the drawing room, a nice long room with soft colors and warming lights. He looked around and then lifted his head to study the portrait that Lawrence Klonaris had done of the three of us. A strange painting. We seemed to be sitting on a high stone wall, a very ancient wall, and behind us the dark landscape dipped down into a far valley with a river that twisted away between huge mountains. The sky was a melancholy gray, broken by a cloud that moved toward us, warning of a storm. Why Klonaris painted us in this setting still causes me to question him and I even complain that, being from a very tropical country myself, I would have preferred him to have depicted us among birds of paradise and palm trees. Strangely, also, he had Charles leaning on the wall, a far-seeing expression in his eyes, and, shirtless. His slight pigeon chest is there, like his father's. Samantha perches beside me in a gypsy dress, looking prepubescent and sulky, and I, central, clasp an amethyst crucifix and look like Mary, Queen of Scots again. The solemnity of my expression in portraits and stills always shocks me.

Tilly says that Finchy stared long and hard at the portrait. It had been four years since he'd seen the children.

"They're my family," he told Tilly.

"I know, master." Tilly still kept that touching and yet embarrassing obeisance in her address. I didn't bother to correct her anymore when she addressed me as Missy Yo. We loved Tilly and I knew that there were some lessons in her that I would never be able to unteach.

Peter stayed under the painting.

"I have to see my family for the last time."

"But they're not here, master."

"I must see them. They're going to kill me."

Tilly gasped. "What does master mean?"

"They've put a voodoo on me."

"What's a voodoo, master?"

Finchy was cold sober. He was standing very still and he looked pale. Tilly stood beside him wringing her hands.

"Oh, master!"

Suddenly Finchy turned to her. "Can't you see him behind me?"

Tilly says he crouched away from the fireplace, pointing his hand over his shoulder. She was scared. Perhaps the madame's master had gone cuckoo. What was he talking like this for? What was voodoo?

"What him, master? There's no him there!" What was wrong with Missy Yo's husband?

"Can't you see him behind me? The black man!"

Tilly let out one of those high, short wails that express absolute terror. She was starting to shake. At the same time, she wanted to help Finchy, so she had to open her eyes and see if there was indeed a black man behind his shoulder. Forcing open her eyes, she stared at the orange wallpaper behind him with the picture of some English cows grazing peacefully on an old farm. Sure as hell, there was no black man there.

"There's nothing there, master. I promise you. On my honor. God help me, master."

Finchy had moved across the room to an armchair that faced the marble fireplace. He carefully sat down.

"I know he's there. They put him on me."

"Oh-oh-oh Jesus!" wailed Tilly. "They've witchcrafted you, man!"

"It's the Jamaicans. The duppies."

Tilly sank to the ground. "Master, please tell me. What is the duppies?"

"Dead people that haunt you. That man behind me."

Tilly started to cry. Like any African girl, she had her own tribal memories of witchcraft and the curses that can be used against the enemy. It seemed even more terrifying that this great white man, this film star, should be speaking of things like that. God help them all. What was she to do?

"The missis is gone out to dinner and the children's at school in the country."

I had put the children at weekly boarding schools at Ascot. The schools were seven minutes from each other and both places were cozy and instructive. They had to learn something sometime and although it broke my heart, I knew in the two pieces of it that I wasn't ever going to be the sort of parent to stand behind them, like the aforedescribed duppy and do the threatening needed at homework time. I'd worked it out that if there was a four-minute nuclear warning, I could don the "phony nurse's" uniform I kept in the closet, put the mock-up emergency Red Cross flag on my mini and hurtle along the pavements onto the Cromwell Road and out to Berkshire, the Cromwell Road being known by people in the know as the road that runs between Harrods and the airport. If I wasn't apprehended by police or shot as a deserter, I could get to them before the bomb hit Piccadilly. At least I'd die in the attempt.

I kept my plan a close secret, knowing how quick people are to get onto a good thing. The schools put the young ones to bed at eight-thirty sharp and the time in London now, at the scene at Launceston Place, was well after ten.

Tilly pulled herself together enough to offer Finchy a drink. Perhaps a little tingle awakened her to the memory that my husband was not averse to the stuff. He accepted a whiskey and poured one for Tilly, who never drank.

Finchy was looking very unhappy, leaning forward in his chair, his head lowered and his hands together. "Will she be late?"

"I don't know, master. She only went out to dinner. Oh, G-G-G-G-Gott man!"

"Can I speak to the children? Telephone them?"

"I don't know, oh master, I don't know. They'll be sleeping now, the poor things. We shouldn't."

They sat in silence, Tilly squatting at Finchy's feet. She would always fall to the ground at the first sign of tension or dissent. At that moment she couldn't have stood up if you'd threatened to kill her.

An hour must have gone by, during which time Finchy repeatedly twisted his head to acknowledge some presence at his back, keeping the almost hysterical Tilly at a pitch of terror she had never before experienced.

Suddenly they heard a car pulling up outside.

"Perhaps that's the missis," Tilly prayed aloud.

The bell rang and someone started to hammer on the door. Finchy and Tilly were shocked into immobility. The battering went on and then a female voice screamed:

"You let him out of there, you white bitch!"

The two figures sat glued.

"I tell you, you white witch. If you don't let him out I'll curse you."

Both of them were shaking now.

"Stay still," Finchy warned.

The haranguing continued at a higher and more determined pitch. "I'm warning you! Open this door!"

The century-old door shuddered under the barrage. Tilly, stunned into disbelief, looked to the master for an order. None was forthcoming.

"What shall I do?" she whispered to him. He shook his head.

"I'll have to answer it. She'll break Missy Yo's door."

"Oh God, oh God!" And that's all he could say.

Tilly got to her feet, her fighting spirit rising to the occasion.

"I can deal with her, master. You just sit there. Crazy woman!"

Tilly tiptoed to the door and released the catch, carefully leaving the chain attached. She faced a furious dark woman who must have suffered a surprise. They glared at each other like a couple of bulldogs on leads.

"Where is he?" demanded the stranger.

"You leave my master alone."

The lady stepped back slightly, then let out a yell. "You get out of there, Finchy. Do you hear me?"

A couple of windows were opened along the quiet Kensington street. A most unusual disturbance!

"You go away and leave that man in peace, you crazy woman!"

"Shut up, you black bitch!"

That was enough for Tilly. She tried to push the door. The woman put her shoulder against it and screamed again.

"You white slut. Let him out of there. You want him now because he's famous. Finchy—do you hear me? I'm coming in to get you."

"No you ain't," responded Tilly, heaving all her strength at the frail wood that separated them.

Finchy hid behind the door of the drawing room.

"He is my missis's husband. Get off with you."

"That white whore. I'll put a curse on her."

"My madame," said Tilly as grandly as she could between huffs, "is not at home."

"She is. She's inside. You better let me in or I'll break this fucking door!"

Several more interested neighbors emerged from their genteel homes for a peek. Apart from young drunks singing their way down to the Cromwell Road after an evening at the pub, the neighborhood never had altercations like this. The noise was appalling, to say nothing of the language.

Finchy decided to face it. He wormed his way to a stance behind Tilly.

"Leave me," he said gently. "I'll be coming back soon."

"You come now, do you hear me. *Now!*"

The woman turned to the black limousine that stood waiting outside the house. A Godfrey Davis driver sat woodenly behind the wheel.

"You come and help me get this man out of there."

"No thank you, madame," he replied.

The woman stuck her arm in the space between the door and the doorjamb and grabbed Finchy's sleeve. She started to tug. Tilly screamed, "Stop that! Do you hear me? You just stop that!"

The chain was pressed to its furthest resistance.

"It's no good," said Finchy. "Take off the chain."

"Are you sure, master? She maybe kill us."

"No, it's all right. Let it off."

Wearily he stood back and Tilly released the chain. She wasn't at all sure they were doing the right thing. The moment the door was opened, the woman took a firm hold of his arm.

"What are you doing here, you cunt! You are coming home, right now!" She started to pull Finchy out of the house. Seeing a black woman treat one of the white giants in this fashion was just too much for Tilly. She grabbed his other arm.

There ensued one of the most extraordinary tugs-of-war ever witnessed by that London borough. Finchy put up no resistance as the two ladies heaved and tugged for possession. I can only thank the Lord Almighty that I didn't get home in time to see the spectacle. As the battle progressed, the language deteriorated. No dulcet speaker at the best of times, Tilly was now letting her formidable voice carry its panic-stricken message far and wide, joined with the stranger's lusty threats and obscenities, the cacophony must have been frightening. The stranger was winning. She had him halfway down the front steps. Tilly was at a worse angle, pulling as she was against gravity. His sleeve split at the shoulder and Tilly lost her hold. He was being dragged toward the railing and gate. With a last attempt to resist the inevitable, Finchy caught hold of the railings with one hand. Tilly bounded down the steps to help. The game was lost and the poor man was thrust head first into the attendant car. The chauffeur had wisely kept his eyes on the road throughout the joust. The big black car disappeared up the street. Tilly closed the door and collapsed onto the floor and that's where I found her fifteen minutes later, weeping her heart out. We held each other after she had blurted out the terrifying tale. I knew I had to find him. If he was in danger from duppies or wild, wild women, he needed me. I started to call all over London and located them at the Dorchester.

"Put me through to the suite," I told the switchboard.

The voice was nasty.

"Could I speak to Peter, please."

"You sure can't," she said. "And leave him alone!"

The line went dead.

When to the sessions of sweet silent thought
I summon a remembrance of things past,
I sigh the lack of many a thing I sought,
And with old woes new my dear time's waste.
Then can I drown an eye, unus'd to flow,
For precious friends in death's dateless night,
And weep afresh love's long since cancell'd woe,
And moan th' expense of many a vanish'd sight.
Then can I grieve at grievances foregone,
And heavily from woe to woe tell o'er

The sad account of fore-bemoaned moan,
Which I now pay as if not payed before,
  But if the while I think on thee, dear friend,
  All losses are restor'd and sorrows end.

Finchy knew that Shakespeare sonnet by heart. I had to look it up.

20

I DIDN'T KNOW what the going price for women was after the divorce. For quite a few years after that. And when I did . . . it was too late and never enough. There was still a woman there, in there somewhere, soft and pliant, juicy and romantic and in dead trouble. I lay on my bed in the afternoons and at night whirled around in the sheets so hurly-burly that in the morning I came to shrouded like a mummy, with my nose pointing toward the dressing table directly opposite the headboard. The whole thing gave me a headache, but I didn't miss Finchy. Not one minute.

Since the divorce, I'd been very careful about trying out a lover at home. I knew that none of them would last, or that some of them might even try to move in. If I'd wanted to be promiscuous just to exorcise Finchy from my body, a stream of different men would be noticed, if not by the beloveds, certainly by Miss Murphy, our seventy-year-old nanny, at that ripe old age still a virgin, although intensely interested in every male who approached our territory, I thought.

I decided to give masturbation a go. My Danish girl friend Lotte told me she made herself come three or four times a day. Naturally, I didn't expect to meet those heights and I understood that the Danes always overdo sex, but I did feel out of things not being able to and bought a baby-blue phallic-shaped vibrator. I tried it once and threw it in my bottom drawer with other useless mementos.

Lotte was delighted to be of help. She brought over with her a handmade dildo. It was enormous, made from a roll of Johnson's cotton wool and covered with a condom.

"But Lot, that's a tool!"

Lotte was a sculptress by trade and the thing looked impressive, even sexy.

"I'm not doing it with that," I said. "It's illegal!"

"Don't be ridiculous. It's just that you're not supposed to travel with them. The customs don't like it."

"No, Lot," I told her crossly. "I want to learn to do it with my fingers. I might be stuck on a desert island one day. I wish my mouth could get there."

"Well, it can't, so forget it."

We lay down beside each other on my bed, naked.

"I always never spend a penny first," said Lotte. "It makes it quicker. With a big bladder."

"How sordid!"

"Yes. Now, watch."

I leaned on my elbow so I could see better. She put her two middle right-hand fingers on the very top of her pussy and began to massage herself gently back and forward. She glanced at me and made a nice little meow sound.

"Are you coming already?" I asked, amazed.

"Mmmmmmmmmm . . ."

Her hand was moving faster and faster and the other had taken hold of a nipple, which she rubbed softly with spittled fingers.

"Mmmmmm . . . I'm coming."

She let out a lovely soft moan and came. It was adorable. No sex, no passion, just a straight autonomous self-frig. I admired it tremendously.

"Is it that easy? Really? Or are you pretending? Lotte, I'm talking to you."

After having done herself, she lay there with her eyes closed, her hand still covering her mount. She looked so happy I decided to give it a whirl, but it looked as though I might not get her full attention for a while. Learning how to do myself, at my age, and to myself, was no easy matter. I couldn't go straight into it like Lotte, who was so sure of her power. When I put my hand down there to feel around, I felt slightly guilty, as if I'd stolen someone's bicycle on a rainy day, but as I played around with myself for a bit, the sun came out and little drops of moisture formed there. I began to rub quite vigorously, producing a not unpleasant buzz around that area, and I turned to Lotte for reassurance. She'd come around and was smiling at me. She leaned down to study the action.

"You haven't got your fingers right on it."

"I have."

"Well, try there and here." She pushed my wrist down a little. "That's better, no?"

"No," I said. "And my hand's tired. I'd rather have a wet dream any day."

"Keep going," urged Lotte. "You have to learn. Imagine going through life without being able to do that for yourself. Worse than death."

I kept going until I couldn't take any more. I was further away from an orgasm than ever.

"Maybe I should try doing it with that thing you made, as well. I'm used to having something there and it might help."

Lotte oiled the dilly and let me have it. Looking at it, I thought she must have a cunt the size of a mare; it was two and a half inches thick, never mind the length, a good twelve. Well, I'd just fiddle around at the opening, so to speak, and see how much of it I could get in.

"And squeeze your bottom and legs, just like you do when you have a man inside you and want to pull him into your heart."

The tip of the dildo felt almost real and Lotte helped me push just a little farther and suddenly I engulfed the magic fraud and came with a brilliant clitoral/vaginal implosion that quivered my every nerve.

"Oooohhhh. Ooohhh, Lotte, oooohhhh! Jesus that's the best I've ever had. Oooohhhh."

Lotte smiled down at me. She was very proud.

"You could make a fortune with those things, Lot," I whispered when I could speak.

"They're dynamite. Much better than a man's and thicker and it doesn't hurt and pull and it's not too big and not too small and you can take it out afterward yourself and wash it and keep it in the drawer for next time."

I happily fondled the disgorged tool. Perhaps I had found the answer to every woman's prayer.

"I think we should patent it, Lot," I said.

I'd gone to Birmingham to shoot a television play. In the hotel gift shop was a gigantic, heavy-lidded, smiling black-and-white-spotted dog, all toy. He looked like Nana, the children's nurse in *Peter Pan.*

I bought him and packaged him and wrote a long card to the children from Finchy. The hotel would arrange to send him a few days before Christmas. I knew I was spoiling the kids, giving in to them always, giving to them too many things and letting them drain me emotionally. I sometimes had the uncertain feeling that they were cannibals, or some other kind of strange creature that smells emotional wounds, senses blood and fear and with some unerring tribal memory, puts in the dagger for a final twist.

Children are not kind.

When the big present arrived from Manchester with the fake letter from Peter, Charles read it, smiled and told me I needn't pretend anymore.

I had acquired for myself a new agent, who was charming, tried like the devil to get me going strong again, to dig a foothold for me in the business and who was fun. His irresistible quality was his dancing. He danced like a dream, Astaire style, and I loved that. We couldn't do what we liked to do in discos; everybody was out there on the floor doing their own thing and if you tried one of Fred and Ginger's back drops, you'd be likely to have your neck broken by a fellow still doing the twist, twenty years late. So off we hustled to the Hammersmith Palais, where everybody was doing it our way and to the sound of an almost living band of musicians. They looked as if they'd been stolen from Madame Tussaud's waxworks, given a shot by Dr. Frankenstein and told to get up there and swing, man. God, it was fun, and Bernie and I had ourselves a ball. He was married, too, of course, and in those days most people were still hanging on. Things have changed.

One night I had a bit of a cold, so Bernie came to see if I was all right. Just watching his dapper, terribly British pin-striped body and polo tie made me feel better. We drank champagne and sent out for Chinese food and had it in my bedroom. I was wearing an ice-blue nightdress and chiffon negligee, terribly seductive and glamorous, because I was pissed off with life and I'd decided to seduce Bernie. After dinner we started to dance, flying around the room; leaping over sofas like nymphs, twirling and encircling each other and feeling marvelously happy. Suddenly, Bernie leapt into the air to perform a rather complicated *pas de deux* in flight, not strictly Astaire, but anything goes when you're with the music. I heard a terrific crack, immediately assuming that someone was shooting Bernie from the pavement. Bernie let out a scream as he lay moaning. I rushed to him.

"I've broken it." Bernie was moaning and flopping from side to side like a landed trout.

"What *are* you talking about? You've been shot."

Bernie shriveled. "Shot as well! Oh, God, my ankle."

"Ankle? What ankle?"

"My broken ankle, you twit. I must have done something while I was up there dancing."

"Now, come on, darling," I said soothingly. "You can't break an ankle in thin air, dear."

"Well, I have and it's fucking painful."

"Oh, my poor darling."

"Get me some cold water, for Christ's sake. The bloody thing's blowing up like a balloon. Oh, Christ!"

"Can you put your arm around my shoulders and we'll hop upstairs? Then we can stick it in the bath. Were you in the war?" I asked Bernie as he yelped and howled his way one flight up. I told him to take off his sock and suggested that he should take off his trousers as well so as not to get them wet. He obliged and as he sat on the arm of a chair, I disrobed him, leaving his shoes, a sock and his pants on the same chair. We hobbled into the bathroom to place his ankle in cold water. After making such a din, I was surprised the children were still so quiet. It was 3 A.M. and I shut the door of my sanctuary. I returned to the patient.

"Shall I get a doctor, Bernie, or what?"

He smiled wanly. "No, it's all right. I've just cracked the fucker. I'll be on a stick for a few days. Nothing serious."

"Oh, my poor darling. How could it have happened?" I sank down beside him as he dangled half of himself over into the cold water. "Let me give you a drink."

"Yes. And I'll have to call my wife."

"Of course, dear. She'll be worried about you." I brought the telephone over to him and he dialed.

"Darling? Frightfully sorry to call so late, but Henry and I got held up with the director after the show. It went well, yes, great, but there's a lot more to be done before it can come into town. Sorry, luv, I'll stay up here tonight. Big kiss, too, good night, darling."

Now, I'm really going to have you, boy. Foot or no foot. And I did.

When Charles and Samantha heard the quietness from the "grown-ups," they crept downstairs to see if I was safely tucked into bed. The angels! I'd locked my door, which immediately brought unknown suspicions to their minds. Charlie bent his little frame to study the keyhole and got a full close-up of Bernie's shoes and socks and pants. He and Samantha climbed upstairs. Sometime later, when Bernie was snoring and I was still smoking and relishing the so recent ecstasy with a virtual stranger *and* an agent, I heard the tapping on the door. What in Christ could anyone want from us now? I wandered through the archway into my boudoir, which was closed off by its sanctuary door. There was actually a little bronze knocker on the other side, with a figure of Satan in battle with righteousness and inscribed underneath with the word "Sanctuary." Everybody took it with a pinch of salt, but I know that I was trying to tell them I was having a battle with myself, wasn't sure who was going to win or whatever, and needed a place of quiet and privacy. Under the door lay a piece of folded paper. Curious, I picked it up and opened it to read:

> Dear Mummy. We love you very much, so please don't do it again, after all, we're only human. Charles and Samantha.

Only human? What was I? Not only human? I could never be only human ever again because of them. Didn't they know I needed a tender heart with someone my own age? That kisses and cuddles and stories for children and the fear for their life and health wasn't enough? That I needed a man, had found a man and was probably going to be so human that I'd give him up for them? Vicious, devilish, children parent-eaters. I shuddered with rage, getting back into bed with Bernie, who still snored. He turned to me to find me again, and I barely resisted, through good manners, kicking him in the broken ankle.

21

THEN ALONG CAME the first man who'd ever told me that he loved me and that I had a brain as well as a cunt. Falling bottomlessly in love with my first Jewish lover, I felt as if a dead weight had been lifted off me. I was grateful. I was damned.

It had been a Monday, probably, and one of those blasting blue days when the rain seems sly and vicious and city people sway in their masses down streets toward their buses and workplaces with last Friday's sweat under their arms. That day, they steamed.

I hurried toward the theater on Shaftesbury Avenue to do my piece in another potboiler signifying nothing, but I was grateful indeed that at least I was back in the profession. "Yolande Finch, er Turner, has returned to the fold, dears. The old boy's gone native! Living rough in Jamaica with *God know's what!* Silly boy. Of course she took him for every penny, didn't you, darling?" Ah yes, each little day was filled with the pin pricks.

On that dying day I walked those streets swaying, toward the evening performance. We'd been going for weeks now; it might have held for a couple of months. Depending on the weather and the tourists. Never, never, did I ever hear anyone in the English theater say, "Look, if it's good, they'll come." It was always touch and go in the commercial theater. Maybe it wasn't like that at the National or at Stratford, but in the West End, it was really the luck of the game, old boy—and *always* use *star* names.

Plays came and went like shadows on a temperamental day. Talk about speculative!

We played the piece to a semi-warm audience and we all knew it wouldn't be long now. Actors sense these things, like sheep at the abattoir. We drearily slouched back to our dressing rooms, we poor players. Nonetheless, it was such a cozy feeling to be working. To know you had somewhere to go every night and twice a week to matinees, to gossip and giggle and tell dirty stories and brag about your pay.

The telephone sounded in the corridor outside my dressing room. I let it ring, knowing that the pounding of feet would quickly extinguish it.

"It's for you." Knuckles hammered on my door.

"All right, all right! Don't break the bloody door down."

"Sucks to you."

I lifted the receiver. It was a friend.

"Do you want to come over and have something to eat?"

"Where are you?"

He named a show business restaurant, The Pickwick.

"Okay. Why not?"

I was drinking harder since I'd lost my alcoholic husband and I needed company to do that.

Jamie didn't look like a Jew, but he walked the way many European Jews walk, with a kind of slouch, as though his knees were too close together, and because he was enormous, he pushed his huge head low down on his shoulders and shoved it forward, which made him look very hostile, if not bloody dangerous. I'd never met Goldner, author of many classic tales, although I knew of him through his work as a writer, as one of the best in the world, they said. When people talked about him, they sounded jealous. He was too smart by half, they said, and he could kill a man with his tongue. And a woman? I'd wondered.

As he lumbered over to our table, I thought to myself, Now, he'd make a great Othello! He nearly did, too, but that was at the end, if there ever is an end to passion.

The introductions were brief and he was abrupt.

"I know Peter."

"Really? How nice."

"He made my first picture for me."

"Oh!"

"Good actor."

"Oh yes. Marvelous!"

"All actors are stupid fuckers."

"I happen to be an actor, Mr. Goldner."

"Then you must be stupid, too." Sharp gray-black eyes. "I've got to go. See you around."

He walked off to another table. I was speechless.

"He's a bit rude, old Jamie," my friend said.

"Rude! He's the rudest, ugliest man I've ever seen. I hope I never have the—I hope I never see him again!"

The following night we became lovers. How can you detest someone on sight and yet know that that monster will teach you more than you ever dreamed existed under the sun?

"I love you, too," he responded after we made love, "but please remember that no matter what happens, there is and never will be any chance of my marriage being affected."

I thought this over. "Not even if she knows?"

"She won't know."

At least he's honest. Like De Sade. Anyway, I hate him really. He's ugly, repulsive and he's so fat! Ugh! He was swinging around in his black leather chair at the apartment, their apartment. Everything was colored either black, brown, orange or white. I sat down on the brown leather sofa. He worshiped my legs with his eyes. That's right, I thought, fall in love with the old pins. They all do. I felt the ladder in my dark stocking creep up to my thigh and watched him watch it.

"So you hated him, did you?"

"Who?"

"Finchy?"

"You're crazy."

"What went wrong, then?"

I fiddled on the sofa. Jamie waited.

"You are a very beautiful girl. What are you doing with your life?"

"I'll think of something. . . . Life's just a way of passing the time anyway."

His eyes scrutinized me while his mouth took on its hard look.

"Well"—I smiled, trying—"I suppose I'd like to be happy."

His look got nastier, but I was thankful that I caught a sadness there and realized suddenly that for him it must be like talking to a backward child.

"If you feel I need analysis . . . I don't feel sick or anything, but if you feel . . . "

"You remind me of Chekhov's heroine in *The Darling*. She could become everything for every man. I don't want you to have analysis for me, luv, but for you."

"But why?" I demanded. "I'm doing all right." Pause. "Aren't I?"

"Are you?"

Was I? I was strong and I had a good cover, always gay, dancing around, being sarcastic, caring not a damn about anybody except my two beloved angels at home. For them I would kill. Wasn't that normal? What was normal? Nobody's going to get me alive. The thought went through my head. Was anybody trying to? I didn't want to think about it.

"I don't really want to think about it."

Jamie roused himself and came toward me. He took me in his arms and I felt safe but afraid. What did he want of me?

"It's the most exciting adventure in the world," he said softly. "The venture into your interior. I think you're worth finding out about, don't you? Then you'll know why you do the things you do."

The next day he bought me Anthony Storr's book called *Human Aggression*. I read it and found a lot in it. Many things about myself. I went to see Dr. Storr and through my smiling anguish and fast talk, he saw the fissures, because at the end, he told me he thought I would benefit from psychotherapy. Psychotherapy! Jesus!

"I don't even know what psychotherapy is, Doctor!"

"Unfortunately, I won't be able to help you myself, but I know a very good man. He's close by where you live—Kensington, isn't it? I'll telephone him."

I drowned in gratitude and showered him with charm and promises that I would get well soon. I'd look up psychotherapy later. Hating him, I walked out of the door. Rejected! Rejected? What was I thinking about? I was going mad already and they hadn't even touched the first layer. God help us all. I prayed without meaning to and to no one all the way back to the house. Our deadly nanny, Miss Murphy, greeted me with the news that Charlie had been rude, the boiler was broken, Samantha had torn up all the family photos, the dog had shit on my new white carpet and, frankly: "Mrs. Finch, if I'd known when I came to you five years ago, I well, dear, wouldn't have stayed."

Stopped dead in my tracks by this lusty seventy-year-old bitch, I remembered wanting to kill her, there and then, with my own hands. Letting the urge pass, I walked through her, asking her yet again not to give me the bad news first. Like father back from the office. Couldn't there be something good that happened all day? Would she try to be a good Catholic and help a friend in need with a funny story, say, a giggle, you know? Something adorable one of them had done, seen? Mounting the stairs, I whispered to her, carefully so that she wouldn't take offense, "Dear Miss Murphy, you are a trial!" I smiled at her gently, walked into my sanctuary, my bedroom and boudoir, where the air was still and only occasional shafts of soft yellow sunlight fell across the book shelves and glass ornaments. Peace.

The children screamed as Miss Murphy tried to persuade them into their coats for a walk around the park. No peace.

Later, Jamie tried to describe to me the reason for our passion. It wasn't really "love," he told me; it was a thing called "collusive transference," a coinage of Freud's to put the guilt on the lily, as usual. I didn't understand what the hell he was talking about, of course, never having taken Freud to heart or head. But I was dying to listen.

"You see, we are not in love with us as grown-ups; we're in love with the image of ourselves at another time in our lives when we were traumatized."

"Come again?"

"Something shocked us as individuals when we were young. They call it a trauma and we see each other in each other as we were then."

"You've got to be joking."

"It's very hard to explain."

"Really!" I exclaimed, "I've never heard such a load of bull in my life. Really!"

Jamie was silent for a little while. Then he sighed.

"Do you really think I'm mad?" I asked him as I sniffed the soft curls on his back.

"You have a long way to go to be nuts, but you're off beam."

"But you do love me, don't you?"

He sighed.

I sat up beside him.

He turned his big dark head away from me and then reached for a cigarette on the bedside table.

"You know," he said when he settled back on his elbows, "that it's very hard to talk to someone who hasn't been through analysis. Very hard."

"Well, it's fucking impossible to talk to someone who has, so we're quits."

"You swear too much."

"You're always sounding like something out of Genesis!" I snapped.

"So when did you hear about Genesis?"

"Look, I may be a Christian, God forbid, but I have met other Jews, you know. In fact, my best friend in Johannesburg was Lucille Sneiderman."

"Nice name."

"She was hideous!"

"Naturally."

He blew the smoke out slowly, turning on his back. The fur on his chest glistened. I touched it.

"Do you know, I've never seen a man with fur on his back?"

"Thereby lies a tale."

"Oh tell, oh tell."

I could lie under his shoulder with my head tucked into his armpit so that he could smoke without knocking me with his elbow every time he took a draw.

"Tell me a story," I asked him. "Tell me a story, please."

"Stories, stories. It's always stories with you."

"Well, I remember you telling me a story about the only way you could fight yourself out of some nasty moment in the barracks room was with words. Wasn't that true? Wasn't it?"

He stroked my shoulder and I did hunger for him.

"Yes, my love, that was true."

"Well—tell me how you got black curls on your back."

Another sigh. Oh how that man could sigh. I waited.

"We were East End Jews, you know?" He bent his head to my upturned eyes.

"Yes? Yes, of course I know that. Where's the East End?"

"Christ, the ignorance of it."

"Well, go on anyway. The place isn't important. Is it?"

"No, Mrs. Kensington, no." He looked at his watch on the bedside table. "You'll have to be off, luv."

I started to sweat. "Why, where is she?"

Jamie pulled his body away from me and wrapped his orange kimono around his enormous frame. A whale, I thought. He looks just like a whale on legs. Slowly he walked out of the room.

"Please, Jamie, tell me a story before I have to go," I whispered to myself.

"I love you," I called out, and he lumbered back into the room and leaned with his elbow against the doorjamb.

"You have a habit of always speaking to me when I am out of

earshot." A troubled, sardonic smile started, and then as he studied my devotion, it changed into the sweet, open grin that tucked the corners of his mouth upward into his cheeks and showed his strong, white, uneven teeth.

"I wonder why."

"I wonder why what?"

"You always talk to me when I am not there?"

"Just wishful thinking, I suppose."

I followed him into the small London bathroom of their flat above Jermyn Street. Oooooh, I did love that apartment. Covet it. I threw her cotton bathrobe off the hook behind the door and kicked it behind the lavatory. He noticed and shook his head. Naughty, naughty.

He started to shower noisily in the bath, asking me through the foam if I wanted to come in.

"No. I want to keep my smell of you."

I wandered back through the short corridor to their bedroom and opened the closet doors. Not many clothes. They had the house-in-the-country-week-end-style-East-End-life. I looked down at their shoes. She only had two pairs, a pair of boots neatly stuffed with plastic muscles and a horrible pair of pink slippers. Motherly, I thought. Denying my urge, I didn't touch anything although my fingernails were curling toward their communal proof of life together, longing to rip it all. Help me, I wailed. I felt very, very evil. I gathered the cold sweat into pools in my palms and dropped them plonk on the carpet. When he came back I was dressed and pretty and had taken a deep gin. I was beginning to appreciate the opiate of the strong stuff. With Finchy it had made me puke my guts out, but now I could throw it down with the best of them.

As all women on the wrong side of the marital tracks know, weekends and holidays are times of torture. It's not the wanting that makes them that; it's the denial from the other side. We could be sick and dying, but lover becomes husband and father on Saturday and Sunday. He's dying for you by Monday and he enjoys a passionate reunion, but personally I was a contemptuous mistress on Mondays, aloof and sulking. This brought on a row and venemous tears and terrible longings for far-off places together and guilts and counterguilts and more pouring out of words to our analysts. Fucking madness, really.

Jamie made a point of not seeing too much of my children and they were not impressed with him. I think he gave them the jitters, being so huge and tall and always on his face a classic Heathcliffe expression. Looking up at it must have been nightmarish. They didn't hang around, but in their own little ways let me know that the man was an enemy as far as they were concerned. I kept the myth going that their own father, Finchy, was alive and well in far-off Jamaica, where they didn't have mail and that's why they never heard from him, although at birthdays and Christmas I cursed him for being such a selfish, or was it vengeful, bastard. I forged, with the help of friends around the world, postcards and presents from him, and the children took it for a few years, at least until Charles could read.

22

I LOATHED Dr. Racker on sight. When he opened the heavy mahogany door on the sixth floor of a dreadful, mangy early-twentieth-century house on a family block, red brick, middle class, a thin street with primping leafless trees, I thought of death. He returned my lackluster appraisal and took one step backwards.

"Shall I come in?" I spat venomously. He didn't reply, but looked instead at his watch. Ah yes, that made me remember. Every fifty minutes with this nut was going to cost me twenty pounds. Three times a week. Forever, maybe. And Wolf had told me he wasn't going to pay, couldn't pay. Some law existed within the mind industry that insisted that each banana case pay his own trip.

I followed him into his chamber, a dry, square room—bare, horrifying. The couch lay in the center like an operating table, facing the long pane of glass through which London's special putty-violet-colored sky looked back at me. Racker's gray plastic armchair matched beautifully, I observed. He pointed toward the open coffin.

"Would you like to lie down?"

"Shall I take off my coat first?"

"If you want to."

You are going to last about five minutes in my life, little man, and they had better be worth talking about. Okay, I'll give you a chance.

I took off my coat and found the solitary chair on the right of the couch to place it on, with my handbag. *Handbag!* Edith Evans and her line twinkled into my mind's eye. *Mind's eye!* Watch it. You'd better watch that.

Settled at last on my back, I took a quick peep at our friend sitting behind me. Why behind me? He was absorbed in the last button of his waistcoast. Beside him sat an ominous little table, flat except for a bump of a notepad and pen.

"This is lovely."

I said it brightly as I always do to the girls of Elizabeth Arden before a massage. I know it makes them feel good.

"Why do you think you need therapy?"

Which answer should I give, I wondered. Decided.

"Because my lover thinks I should have it." Bright as Goldilocks and see what you can do with that, you shrink-shrivel son of a bitch.

Then the silence. Silence and silence and silence. I began to feel the pleasant part of me shake; something underneath was pushing against it. Shoving back, I fought it, thinking, Okay, you bastard, I can hold a silence just as long as you can. It may be my money, but by Christ, it's your time. I lay there for forty minutes and not a word passed between us. I was on the point of blurting, volcanoing with my life, when I heard his voice say, "That'll be all for today, Mrs. Finch." Enraged, I sprang off the dead bed.

"You can't do that! I haven't had any treatment. Are you crazy? You are supposed to help me. What's the matter with you?"

He held out my coat and handbag and made for the door.

"See you on Wednesday same time? Two-thirty. Day after tomorrow."

How can you deal with someone like that? How? I stared at him, amazed at his nerve and more ashamed of myself than I could ever remember and deeply mad with rage.

"Yes, Doctor. Good afternoon."

He opened the door. I thought I could hear plates being moved around in a kitchen somewhere. Must be his home, too! Ye Gods, what was I into? One thing I knew for certain. I was going to resist like hell. Jamie said I would. He said it was proof that I was neurotic. How right he had been. Before I had even started, I had transferred my infantile conflicts right onto dear old Dr. Racker and he didn't deserve it, poor sod.

Somewhere along the line, I became an insomniac. One had to stay awake because of the dreams, the terrible, nauseating dreams. Dreading the night, knowing that that deep murky pool was being stirred slowly to life and was bringing ghastly squirming horrors to the surface for me to see, to live with and fight again.

Myself at twelve in a flowered nightdress, rising out of my thirty-year-old body. I could see the malevolent pretty angel, stepping out onto the carpet beside my paralyzed body and starting suddenly to wreck everything in my room, throwing the telephone to shatter the mirrors, tearing at curtains, scratching and kicking and ripping and then smiling with hate, leaving me and going out of my door to mount the staircase to kill the children. I knew that was what she was going to do.

Waking and screaming without sound, struggling from the bed, running upstairs and finding nothing, only sleeping children. The fear. The fear and not knowing. Could that be me come back to kill? And anyway, I didn't used to be like that when I was twelve. Did I? A killer?

Another dream. As I wake, I turn my head to those mirrors again and see a young baby, a child of six months bound tightly by a soft baby blanket. It's me and an unidentified "they" have tucked my arms under the covering. It's like being buried alive and I can't get my hands free. I look at the child lying there and screaming with rage, a rage that I would never have imagined a child could support. The hands move and struggle underneath, it's too tight; the rage builds. All I feel is hate and hate and hate. At last I pull the tender limbs out of their prison and stretch them in front of my face. I watch them unwind and exercise and feel the release, the strength and the freedom. I wake in fright as the screaming stops. As the child's hand turns once more into my own arm, I reach for the light. There is no child anymore, but I know what anger a baby can feel, a frustration so powerful it can be matched against any man's. I know that way back then I felt passions as strongly as I'll ever feel them again. And I begin to understand.

Jamie was delighted with my learning. As I moved to self-knowledge, we loved ever more and more.

Unfortunately, I didn't become any less jealous of his conjugal status, nor did his jealousy of me abate. Very often we were enemies. But isn't that what love is for, I rationalized—to suffer exquisite despair in the throes of intolerable desire?

Apparently, I was still very ill. I wanted to be married to him. Come live with me and be my love, I begged. He answered with the Songs of Solomon: "Behold thou art fair, my love; behold, thou art fair." It just wasn't good enough.

Dr. Racker and I were discovering large areas of my buried consciousness. I had made the full transference and he had returned the compliment with a full countertransference. Nothing untoward had happened between us during these complex processes. I hadn't desired him physically and he had spared me any abnormal twist in his countertransference. We had, to our utmost fascination, discovered that my neurosis covered the scale of psychological case histories. I was the absolute neurotic. Steadily we ploughed deeper and deeper, always discovering that my subconscious was brilliantly protective. He was one with me now and helped me translate the dreams that plagued me. If, as Freud had suggested, neurosis and analysis are interminable, so is the Oedipus complex, and I had that, too.

I'd always known that I was slightly in love with my father. He was too tall, good-looking and successful not to be in love with. I'd also seen his penis, which was a grand size. He adored me because I was pretty and feminine and danced and sang and sat on his knee and never made him unhappy or asked the wrong questions, like, "Where have you been, Tom?" or, "Do you have to go away again? You just got back!" or, "I love you more than you love me, isn't that true?"

Mother's questions . . . always at the dinner table, in front of three apprehensive children and two quacking black servants in white gloves.

Daddy would rise slowly to carve the whatever, and servant Freddie would carry the plates, followed by Webbie shadowing him with the vegetables. The dogs, two champion Chows and two champion Pekinese, would begin their slight scuffle and growl under the table, and Mother would dig at Father until we could see his hazel eyes bulge slightly. He would then lay down the carving knife and fork, straighten up and hold out his hands, like an evangelist. Mother's tirade would halt for the ritual, and the rest of us would stick out our hands reluctantly, lifting eyes to ceiling.

"May God, protect this chain, this family, this Turnbull family, from evil. Bless us with your love. Nothing can break this chain or any one of us." Everybody squeezed until Daddy let go and seated himself.

"Dinner should have been at eight, Tommy. You know I can't stand it when you're late."

"How was school today, Russell?" he'd ask my elder brother, ignoring her.

"Tommy, I'm speaking to you."

"All right, Daddy."

"Doing well, are you?"

"Yeah." Russell was the eldest son, the one in line to take over, the one in line on the shooting range.

"Is that all you have to say about your last nine hours?" Daddy could be sarcastic.

"You wouldn't be interested, Dad."

"Then why, in your pumpkin-pip head, do you suppose I'm asking you?"

"Oh, do leave him, Tommy. Let's have dinner in peace for once."

I had rounded a perfect crater in my mashed potatoes with a spoon and winked at Webbie to bring over more gravy. Silently he slid around the table to give me more. The food was always good at home, if one ever had the chance to finish it without the tidal wave of rage that seemed to overpower our family at any group encounter, leaving each one of us distraught and drowned. I gobbled fast, knowing it wouldn't be long before it hit tonight. Barry, my younger brother, and I ate quickly, managing angelic smiles at our parents between each swallow. When we went, we wanted to be full in the stomach.

The Turnbull family ate in silence for a few blessed minutes. Mother ate very slowly, putting each forkful into her mouth as if she were poison-taster for a king. It drove us all mad, but we were allowed second helpings waiting for her.

I suppose she was hoping the children would finish quickly and leave her and her husband alone so they could talk things over. The last thing he wanted. We scoffed fresh fruit salad and thick cream while she hypnotically grazed her lips with her barely laden fork. As if she had given a silent order, the dogs under the table would start a slow snarl, whereupon Mummy would stop her movements, turn to Father and attack him with "I told you I can't stand those dogs under my feet while we eat dinner."

That was the signal. He would let out a kick, sending the animals into a frenzied fight. The black faces of the servants would freeze as they backed against the wall, the offspring catatonized into statues while all hell broke loose. My father, man of drama, would push back his armchair, which always fell backward onto Freddie's toe; the dogs, released from the close circle, would break through from beneath the table; and the battle royal commenced. Chow and Pakes flew at each other's necks, shrieks of pain, blood. At that point, Daddy would pick the silver from the tablecloth by handfuls and throw it over his head into the air.

"That's right!" he'd shout. "Kill each other, kill each other." He'd swipe across, knocking wine glasses and dainty dishes, aiming toward Mother usually, who sat proudly like an offended monarch; then he would pinch two handfuls of the back of one of the Chows. Webbie would grab the other Chow, and off they'd go, to fling the dogs into the swimming pool. Father and Webbie would come back roaring with laughter, but we still scattered nervously around the table.

"That'll cool them off, eh, Freddie?"

The other boy grinned back.

"Yes sah!"

"You can go until I ring for you," commanded my mother.

"No way. I'm going into the backyard to have a Kaffir beer with the buggers. Come on, boys."

And her tears would flow and one of us would have to stay with her, bored and boring ourselves to death with her self-pity and our impotent disgust. Once Daddy had gone, I pretended tears and flew upstairs in a phony adolescent grief, so that one of the boys would have to take the shit from her. I would slam my door—so often that a dramatic crack finally climbed up the wall from floor to ceiling—and lock it. Privacy. My dream. Privacy.

23

THERE'S NO PRIVACY in analysis. And there, I suppose, lies the joy and the pain. You can't hide anymore. From yourself, your doctor, your conscious memories and, finally, from your timeless and unconscious truths, the absolute truths that remain behind that protective membrane once penetrated, closed over, but as alive forty years ago as if they had happened a second ago. There is no time nor space in the unconscious, and the power of the impact, the experience, once too intolerable to contain consciously, stays and waits and knocks at the thin separation between the two, like the dim sound of bells through mists from a haunted church. We all live within the sound of those bells and someday, to be saved from the fear of them, we have to walk through that mist, find the church and face the ghost. At least I had to.

Things were beginning to gel. One day I walked out of Rattie's building and standing on the steps was the insipid doorman or porter whose presence had always disturbed me. Perhaps the fact that he must know that I was going upstairs to see the doctor, that head man, that healer of mental illness, that he knew I was sick or neurotic . . . told his wife . . . talked about me . . . knew?

This day, coming out of the iron gates of the elevator and seeing him against the daylight at the opening of the building, I walked toward him, had to, always. But this time when I got to his side, for the first time in all those months of timeless inquiry upstairs, I lifted my previously lowered head and looked at him and saw him and smiled and I saw his face. Our old eyes met, his blue and mine opening, and he smiled at me and spoke the same words that had crossed his lips at every one of our sessions: "Good afternoon, madame." The words I'd dreaded every time, those ordinary words and that ordinary, kind, elderly mouth saying them. Before, they had humiliated me; now, suddenly, miraculously, they were just a greeting, a kindness, an ordinary set of words with no subliminal threat, and I returned his words. It was so easy. I lifted my dark glasses to the top of my head and just drank in his nice, normal features. I was no longer afraid that he could see behind my eyes and realize that a long time ago in my deep soul I had murdered my father.

Minutes earlier, lying on the couch, a little disgruntled, bored and sleepy, a family of London pigeons had flown across the sky outside the window facing me. The silences throughout that afternoon's session seemed interminable. I didn't want to be there with this man behind me, with nothing to say—why should I bother with it anymore? It was a waste of time, money. I felt resentful. The stillness in the room oppressed me. How I wished he would tell me a funny story. I wanted to get up and leave him and get drunk or lost. I wanted to be amused, to live now. He was stopping me. It was all a waste of time. I was better now, two years better. I'd had enough and he'd served his purpose. I'd paid my dues, grown, and now I felt I knew enough about me. I was well enough to go on.

The pigeons flew back across my view. Oh, the boredom of it!

"Did you see the pigeons?" I asked him.

"What makes you ask that question?"

Stupid fucker. What does he mean "What makes you ask that question?" I asked the question because I had seen the pigeons and wanted to know if he had seen the pigeons. My internal temperature rose; I felt prickles of anger underneath somewhere.

"What a stupid reply, 'What's that supposed to mean?' "

Silence.

"Are you trying to suggest—I mean, I know you're mad—I've

always known it. Don't think I didn't hear another patient of yours screaming at you last week as he left, that you were totally out of your skull! A dangerous freak? That you were trying to destroy him. I heard him and I'm glad, because he knew, we all know, that you're a fake. You're nothing. Sick. A liar. Parasite. Hating us because we think we need you, needed you. You pretend to care for fifty stinking minutes what happens to us. You don't give a shit. As soon as you're ready, I get sent away. What if I need fifty-two minutes? I despise you. I hate you. I wish you were dead!"

I lay there in a seething turmoil. He said nothing! I waited for him to protest, to speak the truth, tell me I was wrong and he did care about me. Suddenly I closed my eyes. Ripples of pain and anger began to swirl inside me.

I was somewhere else. I was sitting on the staircase of our family home, Paradise. Hah, Paradise. I was very small, three or four years old. I turned my head as my father reached the balcony above me and started to descend toward me. He was coming from her, from their bedroom. He'd betrayed me again. I hated him. I wanted him to die for it. I was his love, his mistress, and he was never faithful. As he reached me, I took the long knife from behind my back and stabbed him in the throat and as he fell I kept ramming the knife into his head and body, until he lay there, where I had sat and waited. He lay there dead and crumpled, his tall figure covering the seven steps, the last steps. I dropped the knife and looked down at him, the knowledge of my crime gripping my head in a vice. I had killed my beloved father! It was impossible. I couldn't face it.

How much later I came out of the trance I'll never know. Is it relevant? I was back in my own body. I opened my eyes. The realization of my ancient desires and jealousies and of the wish murder I had committed momentarily numbed me. As if I were coming out of an anesthetic, my surroundings slowly redistinguished themselves. I knew that the doctor still sat behind me and I took a deep breath, breathing it out slowly like a revived corpse testing the truth of coming back.

Even as slowly, I let my conscious mind run through the film of my patricide. I had committed the act that I had felt I should commit, that I had enough evil to commit, enough passion. I had lived it again and somehow had opened the dreaded gates and met the ghost. Somewhere in the center between my eyes, where the conscience lives, where even perhaps the soul lives, mists dispersed and walls crumbled and fell into space; it felt as if a warm light had entered in there; freeing my very being. The sense of well being that accompanied this, bounded only by some sort of light, filled me with an amazing sense of wonder. I was beside myself with happiness.

I reflected on my poor mother. I knew what a monster I must have seemed to her, showing her that I loved him passionately, that I detested her because he had chosen wrongly and that I should have been his wife because I was prettier and cleverer and easy for him to manipulate. I was incredulous that a female child could *feel* such things so young. There was still so much to discover, but at least I knew now from where sprung my major trauma, and looking at it once more, I could understand why that little girl had felt like that and I could understand and tolerate her crime. The poor child.

"Doctor?"

"Mmmmmm?"

"I was there. I killed my father."

"Tell me."

I took his hands in mine when we parted and he smiled.

"Thank you."

"We made a major breakthrough. We did well."

"Yes," I laughed. "We did, didn't we?"

24

"O.K. I'll marry you."

I still loved him and I still could never believe him.

"On one condition."

I still worshiped him and would give him the world.

"I'll give up my four children"—he waited—"if you'll give up your two."

That was the bargain. Biblical. Our little fragments of living substance were suspended between us. The image charged me with terrible and powerful emotions. Why not kill them all? I thought. For our love. Kill all six. To prove our love? I laughed.

"But, Jamie, you've got a wife to look after yours; I haven't."

"That's the deal."

My sense organs fought for protection against the excessive hate I felt for him at that moment. There was the split, the difference, the simple and absolute difference between man and woman. The male could trust his mate to bring the fruit to ripe, but the female had cut herself out of the bargain before time began. Nobody could replace the mother yet—and women knew this every day they took off to offices and the vice president's desk. We may today be in a position to embark on a serious discussion that the time and the space of child rearing could, should, be shared, but was that the reality? Always questions.

"Repeat that."

"I never repeat myself."

"Nor complain or explain."

"Correct."

"I think you just killed me."

"Always overreacting."

"Looks like it."

I sank onto the orange carpet on the floor of the studio he had taken for our love nest. Many plans had been laid there and as I fell back and laughed, I thought of the thousands of times I had been, too.

"You Jew."

"You've come a long way in your analysis. Typical regressive tactics." Racism.

"Well, that's what you sound like—Shylock!"

"Frankly, I've changed my mind. I couldn't marry you. You're too stupid!"

"That's what love objects are supposed to be."

He roused himself from beside me on the sofa. Same old sofa as the one he had in the apartment with her. And same colors. But now he was wearing a shocking pink kaftan with purple braid and a hundred and ten buttons down the front, tiny twists of purple silk that he had to thread through their holes. He loved the kaftan but said it made his fingers tired. It reminded me of the famous theatrical dresser, a little old fellow, who dressed the stars at the Old Vic. Apparently not aware of his vocation, God had suffered the poor man to lose both his thumbs in the 1914 war. This didn't hinder him, however, and he became the fastest costume changer in the theater. He was further beloved of all actors for his thumbs-up sign as he wished them well on their entrances. Have you ever seen a thumbs-up sign with no thumbs?

"So Sylvia knows about us?"

"Yes."

"And?"

"I told her I can't live without you."

I ran into his arms.

"Oh, my love, my dear love, I love you more and more." Kissing him, feeling his beautiful wide lips over my mouth, his tongue licking my gums, thrusting into my throat, I sometimes wished I could die under that suffocating mouth, breathing his last breath. Or die under this body, at least, embracing with dreadful passion until the end. I wished, when I loved him most, that he would kill me and let my orgasm come as I shot into the world. The world was too tame for such immortal lovers.

"Did it ever occur to you," I asked Jamie when we met that night, "that the only reason I have loved you so passionately was that I could never have you?"

"I've made my offer," he said. "You can have me."

"My dearest love." I took him into my arms and felt a great tenderness. "If you had to lose your sons to have me, wouldn't you hate me very soon?"

We lay together, closer than we'd ever been. Only our outer skins stopped us from merging into one complete human.

"I already hate you, my love, and I know that only by loving you I could even have imagined the sacrifice of my children."

I decided to leave with Charles and Samantha for the farthest place on earth, described by ultra travel agents as the Real Beachcomber's Last Paradise. On a kind of "pay till you die" scheme, I booked us out there for two weeks. The flight was miraculous. Cairo Airport was dizzy with tanks and patrols and antiaircraft guns. We trotted off our plane thrillingly covered by nasty-looking men at arms holding machine guns at our stomachs. It was midnight as we arrived and the long beams of searchlights skimmed across the sky searching for one of the dazzling Israeli attacks, which deep in my heart I longed to happen. If I'd been alone, of course. Without Charles and Samantha. But if I'd been alone, how I would have loved to die right in the middle of a gigantic air raid, standing right on the field and watching them hit. I've never seen a war, but I've yet to meet a man who was out there in one of the big ones that didn't say it was the best time of his life. You can't get better recommendation than that. Except for Finchy, but he was different, after all.

Even more enthralling, as we tottered into the lounge, was the sight of about ten thousand bodies walking around swathed in white cotton. The travelers to Mecca. We were given ten minutes to stare at one another and then we were ordered back to the plane, but it was an exciting experience.

As we skimmed across the Indian Ocean at dawn toward the tiny green island, I could see that the description of the place by the agents could tally with the reality. The one catch was that the only hotel already built had triple-booked, a malicious plan arranged by a desk clerk who had been fired and was getting back. There developed a battle royal in and around the lobby of the hotel, human nature at its best, fighting for its entitlement. There was nothing anybody could do about it, so a few hundred disgusted "real beachcombers" had to sleep on the sand for a couple of nights.

Well, that's what we'd come for, wasn't it? Like hell it was. As for me, I was so happy to be out of reach of the man I loved so that he could really suffer, I didn't give a damn. And besides, I watched a pregnant turtle rise out of the sea and drag herself up the beach to dig and lay her eggs. Seemingly hours later, the exhausted matron, having carefully covered her offspring, as slow as fate, made her way back into the ocean. She never looked back, knowing in a memory that spanned millions of ages, that there was nothing more she could do for them now.

At last, we intrepid travelers were safe in air-conditioned rooms with bathrooms and bars and lush lawns outside our glass doors where we could sit and drink and look at the sea. I didn't talk to any of the others on the tour; they looked and sounded like a bunch of rich plumbers from Manchester, old English retired couples and jittery British *nouveaux riches* who carried bundles of notes in their swimming trunks. I lay back in my sunchair, a bottle of champagne beside me, and gave myself to the sun.

One day a little girl came up and I heard her soft voice. "Mam want to buy seashells?" I opened my eyes and there was ten-year-old Charlotte, in rags, with a basket of jewel shells. She was motley colored as if she'd had a skin disease, she was thin, she had twelve little pigtails that stuck out all over her head like antennas and she smiled like an angel. We talked for a little and she told me she and her brother made their life this way. I told her she was selling too cheap and we went into business. I bought the three biggest and most beautiful of these incredible and rare shells and took them with me into the dining room at lunchtime, displaying them ostentatiously on the table. Naturally, everyone wanted shells, so where was the little girl? I told them she and her brother were there every day, but only between ten and one, and he who did not buy would regret it all his life. The greed for acquisition won over past experiences of trying to pack a bloody great conch and then what the hell to do with it when you got back to Llandudno or Jonkers. From then on, Charlotte and frère Jacques were tycoons. There weren't enough shells in the sea for them to sell. Charlotte sold seashells along the Seychelles seashore and she would do all right for a long time or until the nuns found out.

It was macabre to see a cluster of gowned, barefooted nuns beachcombing every morning, like a grounded flock of some displaced sea birds that had lost the know-how to fly. Suddenly, from behind me, through the narrow hotel and back in the jungle somewhere came this long, wild, animal scream. It shook me enough to make me sit up. It rang out again and again. I heard and felt it so strongly that I could almost see it, but what was it and who was doing it and, worst of all, why? I decided to believe it must be some kind of animal, a Seychellses mad baboon or hyena, and dipped back into my room for my earplugs, filled my glass and tried to concentrate on the vista. It pierced through the beeswax and I pushed the plugs farther in.

There are some things we can't escape and for me the scream was going to be one of them. A skinny mediocrity with a beard was strolling toward me.

"Can you hear it? Can you hear it?" I asked him, jumping to my feet.

"Hear wot?" His face took on the numbskull look of a house painter who's got to the top of his ladder and realized he's left the paint on the pavement.

"The scream! You must hear it!" I was pointing backward

toward the unknown other side of civilization. There was a silence. No scream. There you go, just like when you have gotten your dying kid to the hospital and he says he hasn't got a pain anymore.

The beard stared at me, cocking his head, trying his best. His eyes met mine suspiciously and took in the bucket of champagne. I doubted myself, too. The scream had gone.

"Sorry," I said. "I must have imagined it."

"Yeah, well." He shook his head slowly, taking me in. Thoughts of madness plummeted around inside my head for a second as I watched him retreat and then I heard it again.

"Oh my God!" I remember gasping. It was there all right. I looked at the man's back. He was strolling along kicking the sand. I started to walk toward the sound, wishing I wasn't alone, always alone. Hating Jamie and husbands and women who had them, I even wavered for a second. Perhaps I should tell the manager, but the image of his infinitely stupid, greedy face deterred me. I crossed the dirt track road behind the hotel and faced, literally, a jungle, thick with tropical plants covered by creepers and darkened by giant trees that hung with God only knew what kind of vegetation or, Christ! snakes. A small track led into the bloody mess of nature at her worst and I followed it, tracking down the screaming.

The child, a girl of about eight, was in a cage. Ten by ten feet of bared ground were fenced in, holding the prisoner. Farther on was the shanty home. Transfixed, I watched as the child let out one piercing scream after another, naked and flinging herself against the netting, then crouching, then leaping into the branch of a tree that hung above her, snatching its leaves and eating them. On the outside, other native children laughed and shouted at her, throwing stones and fruits and twigs, poking at her through the fence. I hit one with the flat of my hand and sent it sprawling. The others fled behind dim bushes and the girl kept up the ghastly sound. What pain did she have? There must be pain to scream like that. The horror of finding a child in a cage hazed my vision. I couldn't see her face, I only knew that the nightmare was real.

What would Finchy have done? Or Jamie or Jesus Christ? As for me, my blood ran cold and a ringing fear shook my body until at least I was able to find my feet and run to the shack. I hammered on the slatted door and hammered and hammered. An apparition appeared, a woman, white, with a halo of bleached ginger hair. She looked at me impassively, like some tired ghost.

"What is that child doing in the cage? Answer me!" I was panting with grief and horror and fear.

The woman moved her hands together in front of her swollen floral-covered stomach, and her worn young-old face—how could I see her age, so blind was my fury?—her face showed a misty, tragic loneliness and despair. I pushed her and she fell back a little into the dark within.

"You come out of there and tell me what that child is doing in that cage. Do you hear me? Or I'll . . ." What? Or I'll what? My tears started to flow as hers did.

"She mad," the woman said.

"What do you mean, 'She's mad'? Get a doctor. We can't leave her there! How could you do this." My words were falling out, meaningless and echoing between us. "My God, a child in a cage . . . never thought . . . that anyone now, these days!" I took her by the shoulders and shook her. "It's the twentieth century! Don't you know that? Are you a maniac!" Her sobs shook her, and my nose was running and I was wiping it with the back of my hand and the child went on screaming.

"She always been mad. Since a baby. We have to keep her like that."

I started to run back down the path to the hotel. Stinking fear-sweat poured through my pores as I flew into the lobby and to the desk. "Get me the manager and I want a doctor. Immediately. There's a child caged back there."

The incredible passivity of expression that a long-suppressed people can accomplish had previously in my life interested me only theoretically. In South Africa, for instance, where the black could protect himself only with a blank face, a sort of façade or implication of innocence behind which God knows what terrors threatened his brain. Now, as the clerk looked back at my hysterical features, I saw it again. But he had heard me.

"The manager is not here."

"Well, who's the best doctor on this fucking Paradise? I want him. Do you understand?" I said more slowly, "I want that doctor. Get him on the phone."

Like a puppet he walked to the telephone and dialed. He handed me the telephone.

"Is this the doctor?"

There was a silence and then I heard a cough and a slurred Irish voice. "It is." He was drunk.

"I'm at the Reef Hotel. You must come right away. There's a child in a cage."

I heard him cough and spit.

"Do you hear me?" I shouted.

By now various interested guests were gathering about. I wished they would piss off. "Doctor? Do you hear me? You've got to get here. We must do something!"

Silence. Then, "Listen, madame," said the drunken voice, "there's a thousand kids like that all over the island. So don't worry yourself."

"You can't mean that. I don't believe it!" I started to cry.

"Now, now, don't cry. It's a primitive island you're on. Enjoy your holiday." I heard the click as he cut me off. I lay my head on the desk and wept, wracked with the shame of the human race. Someone took me to the bar and I drank a double. A voice said, "You mustn't take these things so seriously. They're only natives, you know. They don't know any better." I left to go to look for the nuns.

As if waiting for me, they stood like a motionless tableau on the fringe of the sea. Charlotte of the seashells sat at their feet drawing in the sand. They watched me approach. The tears had stopped now and all I felt was a terrible weakness and a heaviness in my flesh. There were seven of them, white nuns, young and pink-cheeked and barefoot. Their pale habits moved gently in the sea breeze. One of them stepped a foot forward to meet me. I looked into her face and saw the clear eyes, the lack of guilt. Wearily I asked her if she knew about the little girl. You do, don't you, I thought. You know about them all and it's written, isn't it? Suffer little children to come unto your husband. You do your best, but God works in mysterious ways. Right?

"We visit them and try to help. We know Sarah, she's one of our favorites."

"Are there no hospitals?"

"There's one."

"I could take her back to England with me. Find out what's wrong with her. We have charities for sick children." I was sinking.

"Could you take back five hundred?" She asked it gently, so gently.

I shook my head and knew it was all useless and hopeless and that I was full of shit. I mumbled something about the doctor and she replied that he was a good Irish doctor and he was doing his best, too, although, she smiled, sometimes it got to him and he drank. I thanked her and nodded to the group. How strong their faith must be to survive the horrors of hell on earth, and I felt sick with my own sentiments and hollow compassion. They were in the field and I was dung. Rightly, they had flung me from their hands.

On the last night before departure, I recognized the face of the woman that all along my memory told me I knew. She was the only pretty woman there and walked tall and looked classy. Her husband or lover or mate was treating her like a queen, opening doors and walking behind her like her privileged courtier. The face, though, I knew or had known, but I remembered it fatter, and the body, now slender as a dancer's, had been fatter, more loose. Then, as she walked out of the dining room, it hit me. She was my old friend Marianne, the nice whore with big tits back there in the warehouse when Finchy had tried to turn Convent Garden into Tahiti with us three women. She looked great and I wondered what had happened to her little bastard. My fatherless two were beside me and as I looked at their happy faces, I felt her turn to me and she knew I remembered, too.

Her man came across to us after dinner as we sat having coffee and watching. Always watching on holidays, like refugees. There ought to be an Anti-Holiday Anonymous to get people off it, the sham of strange places with people you wouldn't normally touch. Would I join him and his wife for a líqueur? I'd love to. She had guts, that chickadee. He introduced her as Norma Walsh and I said I was Yolande and sat down. Norma and I touched hands and she gave me a tickle on my inner palm and then put her finger in front of her mouth to show me I better shut up. I shut up and also had the fun of remembering silently with an old friend the memories of times past and in another country.

Late that night we all went swimming in the nude, the three of us, and as I saw her lover making love to her under the water and her arm waving me to come over and join them, I knew that nothing changes and that there is nothing new under the sun.

25

THE LADY at the corner paper shop told me one day she'd heard, that Finchy had taken a flat around the corner.

"Have you seen him?" I asked her.

"No, dear," she replied kindly. "The lady at the candle shop told me." She slowly shook her thin old white head. "It's a shame, isn't it dear?"

"What?" I had to ask back. It was a shame about so many things.

"About him and 'er."

"What do you mean?"

"'Er being black and that. And such a handsome man he was too, dear."

"Well, perhaps he wants to protect her?" A bit cunning, but charitable.

"Well, we're certainly doin' that here, luv! Got the 'ole bleedin' world livin' off us now. Don't 'ave to travel nowadays, girl; you can see 'em all on the Gloucester Road."

"Somebody had to take them in," I said thoughtfully. "They would have been murdered in their own countries."

"Yeah, well . . . it's all very well . . . but. Not that I have any racial problems, dear, it's just you never 'ardly see any whites in 'ere anymore. It's funny, like, you know, dear?"

"The whole world seems a right bloody mess to me," I said.

I loved talking to Londoners. Because they take such a dim view of it all, they turned the other cheek and made a little joke instead of putting the boot in. During the last world war they called it "putting a good face on things." While the blitz was raging over London, a BBC reporter arrived at the scene of an immediate hit, which had rammed to the ground a little row of working-class houses in Battersea. Recording his impressions of the chaos for the world to hear, he was astonished to see a very frail and dusty old lady pulling herself out from under a rubble that had been her abode. He rushed to her, helped her to her feet and thrust the microphone at her. After asking if she was all right and being reassured that "Yes, dearie, never you mind. Me sister was blown through her window with 'er piana last night!" the reporter asked her what she really thought about the blitz. She paused and dusted herself down a bit and then replied, "Well, it takes your mind off the war, doesn't it, dear?"

That sort of attitude was, if a trifle eccentric, always a help to the morale. A sort of "He must know what he's doing, luv," with a glance upward, "or we wouldn't be 'ere, would we?" I myself took 'im for granted, too, in those days. The insidious influence of the other one, Satan, never entered my head.

"Can you try and find out where Mr. Finch is?" I asked her.

"Don't you see him then, dear?" She was dumbfounded. "And those lovely kiddies and all?"

"No."

"Men. They're all the same. Bastards."

"Well, if you see him . . . I mean, if he comes in here, would you tell him we'd like to see him, please?"

"Of course, luv. Shocking, that's what I call it. Shocking."

When I got home I telephoned Ma and got Flavia, the stepsister. She was as cold as ice, sounding happy to be able to repay me for taking him from her. I managed to tell her what I'd heard and asked her to try to arrange that the children see him. Later that evening Peter called and said the children could come out to the studios and see him on the set of *Bequest to the Nation,* a picture he was making with Glenda Jackson. I was terribly happy at his promise and we set the date. Miss Murphy would take them out to Pinewood and they could have lunch with him. Stupidly, I told the children. They were thrilled and we planned what they would wear and spoke of how wonderful it would be to see him again and how proud he would be of them. Only three days to go. It had been five years since they had met. Perhaps they could bridge the chasm.

Wednesday night came. The call from Flavia. Abruptly she informed me that the plan was off. It wasn't convenient. He didn't want it.

"You mean he doesn't want to see his own children."

"I'm just telling you, it's off."

I put the telephone down and burst into tears. Suddenly and incredibly late, I realized that Finchy wanted to punish me and had found the killer weapon. He could destroy me through rejecting our babies. Even knowing the reasons why, because of his own suffering, I wept for Samantha and Charles and swore a dying allegiance with them—that somehow I would try to be their mother and their father. Their shock at his final rejection was heartbreaking.

I worked religiously to keep up the myth that he really loved them so much he couldn't face seeing them. For years I kept his photographs around the house and talked about him as if he was still part of us. It was energy not wasted, but it never fooled them, and the double-edge sword was turned often in my entrails. They loved me, of course, but what had I done to their father to make him run away from us? They hated me for that.

As for me, another devil manifested itself. I was a failure. I was cursed to submerge myself entirely into the horrendous task of bringing them up alone. Of course, I kept up the necessary act, the gay optimist, to make life tolerable for them and to make myself desirable to the world. I took care of my outward self and let no cracks show. I was an enigma. Never appearing a day older as time went by with the painless assistance of daily doses of hormones, keeping my body slender as a seventeen-year-old's, my hair shiny, my nails long. The impeccable woman, desirable and infinitely alone.

If the fifties had been fun and the sixties had been wild, the seventies were scary. Morosity opened the curtains on a decade of frustrations, bankruptcy and migration and sometimes all three. The Labour government slithered into power and bled us dry. The once-great Britain, in the flash of an eyelid, had become Europe's poor cousin and Britain had never even accepted that we were related. True to form, we ourselves did a lot of our own putting down, but with an uncomfortable ambivalence. After all, we had won the war, hadn't we? How come Germany was now the Lady Bountiful? Emotionally—and nations have feelings—it was unjust. Should the victors be vanquished? A grumbling apathy settled on the British, whose indefatigable spirit deteriorated into bitterness, deep cynicism and black humor. "Will the last businessman to leave London please put out the lights!"

Careful on the subject of communism, rumors flourished about Reds under beds, in high places and very probably in the ruling party itself. The unions grabbed the reins, and strikes abounded, swatting the people with no garbage collections, no electricity, no transport, no production. Historically, Britain had the reputation for uniting, even enjoying the challenge of chaos. Now, nobody gave a damn. Like an old lady with a glorious past, we sat on a wooden bench in the park and watched the pigeons shitting on the church. There were some Britons who, in the privacy of their homes, did mumble that we should have had a proper Revolution, like the French had had, instead of the cool Industrial churn-up we had allowed. Perhaps even now it wasn't too late to let the streets run with blood. Ex-colonels screeched about bringing the troops in, but most of the troops were up in Ireland trying to suppress the naughty Irish. The whole thing was "unseemly." Suddenly, there was no "man in the street" to refer to and if there was, he came from Nigeria or Bangladesh. We seduced ourselves into materialism and if the state would pick up the tab for Mr. Jones who stayed away from work, he could watch the new TV, and his wife could enjoy her first washing machine. Inflation was something that happened to balloons. Britain took to the bottle.

Manifestations of the class struggle became very real. Rolls-Royces were assaulted, milk bottles were flung through the serene windows of Conservative MPs' houses, white paint spelled out that anyone who lived in Kensington was a fascist pig. Crippling taxes propelled thousands of the best brains overseas, which was just, some suggested, what Russia wanted. "It'll be easier for them just to walk in and take over, see?"

Finchy had gone to Nassau and Jamaica way back in sixty-eight, which made me suspect that I was not the only reason for his exile. Jamie and other writers had chosen southern Ireland, where artists were treated with more respect; the footballers were emigrating and to make the exodus complete, the Beatles took off. We certainly were cutting off our nose to spite our face.

I was up to my knickers in debt. My alimony, classed as "unearned income"—little did they know—was taxed at 87 percent, and everything I earned above that in the theater or TV was similarly abused. Downright official theft. When some cool criminals made a substantial coup in the great train robbery, we all rejoiced. Being bent was becoming the only way of making an honest living.

I thought about marrying again, but like Tamara, I didn't. Couldn't face another disaster. One marriage to Finchybags was enough. It concerned me that Charles had no male-figure to adhere to and that Samantha didn't have a worshiping father to cuddle her and tell her she was the most beautiful little girl in the world. But deeply I believed that pretty stories about happy families were propaganda to keep society in its place. I didn't know any happy families, but sometimes the advertisements got to me and I cried. One night, I decided that the three of us should make a run for it, to Rome, or New York, or bloody Bali. Then Fate took a hand.

Like most of us, I was always looking out of the side of my eye for the bluebird, commonly referred to as "happiness" or "my real love," the one I was going to get old with and push along on Brighton pier in his wheelchair when we were ninety-five. Ah, fairy tales! He wasn't presenting himself. One woman told me she'd gone to Kenya to find one, because they were all real men there, and there were fifteen of them to one girl. She'd got herself one, but I noticed she never said a word to him all evening, never even glanced at him, and he stood very near the drinks table. It was easy to see what his first love was.

At a cocktail party I glanced up after grabbing another glass of bubbly from the tray whirling by to see across the room a handsome, powerful-looking man replace his finished glass and grab another from the same marathon waiter. Fascinated, I observed us both putting them back, drink for drink, for quite some minutes, until our host, observing, I suppose, that we were two people in dire trouble, introduced us. It didn't take me long to understand that he was drinking away his boredom. I discovered that he was a very powerful businessman, with a heroic past and a name that was a household word. It wasn't that I wasn't impressed, but I felt, because of his immediate attention, and the fact that I was not swooning with pleasure at making his acquaintance, ironically elevated in his esteem. He asked me out to dinner and I refused, too tired to conceive of another relationship with another man. He pursued me in a gentlemanly fashion over the telephone for a few weeks. My mind was mostly concerned about how to escape from England to some tax haven, Switzerland excluded, and hang around a beach or work in a café.

Finally, I accepted a dinner and the great man came to collect me in his Rolls. He met the children whose reaction to him charmed him and amazed me. Very soon, all my debts were paid and we were practically inseparable. He loved me and the children and was a rather magnificent fairy godfather. Once again, I slipped thoughtlessly into the role of "love object" and it was very comfortable to be protected and cared for. Charles and Samantha thought he was perfect and I admired him and respected him, quite the best sentiments to enjoy in a love relationship. I don't think many women would have resisted him and he was certainly the first lover who came close to my dreams of a knight in shining armor. Of course, he was at least thirty years older than I was, but try and find a young guardian angel!

26

DESPITE THE MOMENTARY ALLEVIATION of my penury and loneliness, I was determined to reunite Finchy with his children. I sent a cable to Bertie and Lorrie warning them to be prepared for our arrival and requesting that they approach Finchy discreetly, if at all, at that stage. Blinded by illusions, I was quite sure that by coming upon him at Rossati's a magnificent reunion would occur, rather like the one he had played with his own Ma after years of exile. Falling into my own trap once again, I leveled with the children, whose interest in their dear father was declining at a disturbing rate. Too many other children had asked why they never saw Peter Finch visiting the schools for plays, open days, award givings and other celebrations. Predictably, they hated having to come up with lies to satisfy their friends' curiosity. "I *wish* your daddy would come and see you, Samantha. Mummy, Daddy and I watched him in *The Nun's Story* last Saturday and he was marvelous. Why don't you go and see him in Hollywood?" Or, "Charles, you never seem to get any letters from *your* daddy!" Samantha and Charles were fed to the teeth with having a father who was a publicly acclaimed man who "you can see by his acting, is a man of *great* compassion," when actually Finchy was proving as negligent as any one of his protectors had been to him as a child.

We arrived at Fumencino airport in Rome at eight-thirty in the evening. Things boded well as, through the windows, we saw the late sunset painting the plains around the airport in that glorious Etruscan bronze-pink that looks as if a golden-white saint will rise from the clouds to wave blessings and choirs of angels will sing.

The nonchalance with which I approached the telephone to call Bertie when I discovered there was no one to meet us, only confirms one of the better sides of my nature—sublime confidence. There was no reply.

I stared at the instrument for a little, like a baboon that's been given a wooden banana, and then tried again. There was no reply. Having assumed that the Whitings would put us up for the couple of nights it would take to pursue the vagrant parent, it hadn't occurred to me that they might be away. Cautiously, I counted the money in my purse and dragged together barely twenty dollars. I cursed my impulsiveness but immediately put into effect the attitude of gay abandon that had saved me many a time in the past.

When Finchy and I had been together in Rome, we had always shacked up at the Hasler Hotel. The only thing to do was to go right there. Chop-Chop. I bundled the orphans into a cab and instructed the driver without divulging the state of our finances, to take us to the Hasler.

As we plodded into Rome behind the million cars that preceded us, I noticed Charles becoming restless and, horror of horrors, begin to burrow in the suitcases and zip bags under our feet. I knew by now that if he was on a search for something, he wouldn't stop until every piece of clothing, every possession, was evacuated from its resting place and left where it fell.

"Stop it," I told him. Of course he didn't.

"Stop it, Charles," said Samantha sternly. She knew, too.

"What are you looking for? And please, don't start that now."

Charles turned frantic eyes to me. "Teddy."

"What? Oh no!"

"Where's Teddy? I can't find him."

My heart lurched. Teddy was to Charles what Charles was to me. Indispensable. That teddy bear had rested in Charles's arms as Charles had rested in someone else's arms for well nigh twelve years, through thick and thin, rough and smooth. We had to find him.

"We must have left him at the airport."

He was starting to tremble, little pools of water damning in the corner of his eyes. I didn't hesitate.

"Please take us back to the airport," I nervously asked the driver in bad Italian. "We've lost our teddy bear."

This announcement caused almost one of the nastiest crashes that would ever be witnessed on the route to Roma. The driver slammed on his brakes, forcing the vehicles following to take evasive action, which, as I looked back, made the queue look like the spine of some filleted fish. Then he turned to berate me in hysterical display, screaming and pulling out chunks of hair, hitting his head and jabbing his fat fingers and using what sounded like interesting obscenities to convey that there was no way he was going back to the airport for whatever reason, especially for "a tiddy beel." Samantha burst into tears and Charles sank into a tragic moaning loneliness. My hackles rose with my voice.

"Take us back!"

"No, signora. No! No! No!"

The noise from behind was deafening.

"You must."

"*Non possibile!* Non! Non! Non!"

"Please!" I was starting to whimper, too.

"I canta getta acrossa to that roada, signora! *Impossibile!*"

I saw his point. The returning road was separated from us by a dividing wall.

"Please try!" It wasn't fair on him, but my future life was not worth living if Charles didn't have Teddy.

"Non!"

Charles would have to face the loss.

"We can't go back," I told him. "You should have thought about it in the first place. Why didn't you keep him with you? You're always losing things. If you were more careful and didn't expect me to be there to always pick up after your things, you wouldn't have lost Teddy. Now, you'll have to forget it and it's all your fault."

Charles stopped moaning. He looked at me with malignant distaste. "God," he said, "I hate you."

That stopped me momentarily. How could Charles hate me? I was everything to him! He adored me, worshiped me. He'd even told me once he loved me more than God! I glared back at him, wondering whether I should slap his face and take the risk of getting a punch from Samantha, or enjoy the first pure emotion that I felt. I decided to enjoy the emotion.

"And, God," I returned to Charlie, "I hate you, too."

It was out. The beautiful sound of it. Hate. We had told an absolute truth to each other, and the glorious release lit up my spirit to no end. Charles looked surprised.

"Isn't it marvelous, darling, that we can at last say that to one another after all these years of pretending that we loved each other every single second, which we didn't sometimes?" I leaned forward to take him in my arms if he would let me. He'd started to smile, so I moved over toward him for a kiss and released the hidden Teddy from under my behind.

"You are the end, Mammy," admonished Samantha, who always pronounced it "Mammy," making me feel like Al Jolson's mother. "You were sitting on him all the time!"

I told the taxi driver, who was relieved, if not amused, that we had discovered the "tiddy beel" under my botty, and the caravan of traffic commenced again with the three of us, at least, in high spirits and full of the joys of the adventure.

Arriving at the impressive Hasler overlooking the Spanish Steps, I prudently asked the by-now-resigned driver to wait and hurtled through to the front desk and explained our dilemma to the manager, who thankfully remembered us. Wringing his hands, he explained that not only was his establishment chockablock full, but that the entire city was bursting at the seams because of the various religious conventions taking place that very day.

"But where will we sleep?" I was beginning to feel extremely nervous again and weepy. Everything was going wrong. "And the poor children."

Every Italian becomes inflamed with pity at the mention of children. He did, too.

"Don't worry, signora. Something will be found for you and the *bambini.*"

"A maid's room would do," I told him, never forgetting the present realities. "Or a chauffeur's room?"

"Please attend a few moments and I will try to find something."

I waited biting my nails and praying until he returned.

"God is good, signora. We have found you the only room in the city."

"Oh, thank God."

As he took me to the car, I thanked him, explaining that anything would do; simply anything.

He chucked the children under their chins and my thoughts were again confirmed about the kindness of Italians until I heard him order the driver to "take the charming signora and her beautiful *bambini* to the Grand Hotel." The *Grand Hotel!* Oh my God! How was I ever going to pay the Grand Hotel? With a fluttering heart, and no alternative, I prayed as we were driven to the grandest hotel in Rome.

The handsome young undermanager greeted us like royalty, which should have made me suspicious. As we rose with him in the golden lift, he murmured charming things about this and that and I listened with half an ear, the other half being taken up with counting the twenty dollars in my bag. The escalator rested gently onto the destined floor and we followed behind him to a pair of gold-leafed doors that he proceeded to open.

"The Royal Suite, signora."

I was too shocked to utter. The children ran into the magnificent apartment, glutted with pink roses and antiques, a roaring fire in the marble fireplace between two palatial windows that looked out onto one of the world's most beautiful Bernini fountains.

"Welcome to the Grand, signora."

I thought it wise, whatever the consequences, to take the bull by the horns.

"I . . . er . . . we, haven't got enough money for this. I can't . . . um . . . you see . . ."

A lady's maid and a dignified white-coated gentleman servant had entered, wreathed in smiles. I lowered my voice and drew the undermanager toward the window.

"We were expecting—you see, we've just come from Spain—I was hoping friends—looking for my husband—I haven't any money." It was out. It would be seconds before we were, too.

The manager turned to the couple.

"The signora and her children are very tired and I'm sure hungry. Please see that they have everything they want."

I stared at him. Was he deaf?

"But, you see . . ." By now Charles and Samantha had found treasures in the rooms off the salon. I heard their laughter and the sound of baths being run. The waiter handed me a glass of champagne, which I held like a hand grenade.

"Relax, signora," said the angel. Have a good dinner and a good night's sleep and we'll talk about it tomorrow."

"But . . ."

"Or the next day." He flashed me a loving smile and was gone. I couldn't believe it. They were going to let us stay and they knew I didn't have any money. Who else but the Italians would do that? It was almost a religious experience. When I caught the eye of the man-in-waiting, I saw such a sweetness in his expression, that I knew he understood everything and that, for the moment at least, we were safe. After dinner and bubble baths, we snuggled down in Royal beds and slept the sleep of the blessed. Tomorrow was another day, after all.

We never found Finchy, which taught me not to listen to easy talk. Bertie and Lorrie were away at the lakes, so we never saw them. The Grand gave us spending money to buy little things that can't be resisted in Rome and charged me a ridiculously low price for the three days in the "only room in Rome," allowing me to pay from London. They still send me a card every year to remind me that they're still there.

I punished myself by joining the cast of a revival of Noel Coward's *Design for Living* starring Vanessa Redgrave. Knowing Vanessa had a reputation for taking off frequently on her marches and protests, I accepted understudying her as well. Now, although the Noel Coward/Gertrude Lawrence style of comedy had gone out with high button boots, there can be no denying that Noel Coward at least wrote to amuse however ironic, tragic or even bitter his situations were.

This play is one of his most sophisticated comedies, concerning itself with the permutations within a *ménage à trois,* and was embarked upon with a heavy seriousness that would have lain happier on Richard III. Our director, Michael Blakemore, seemed mesmerized by Vanessa's interpretation of the heroine, and although the two actors who satellited the star tried very hard at first to invest their performances with a certain lightness, they were soon discouraged. The rest of us, cast as three glittering and superficial socialites and a deranged maid, played our parts as they were written, for comedy, but against the wooden tragedy that preceded our scenes, we came off looking like clowns and jesters, with much embarrassment and unhappiness. Furthermore, offstage, Vanessa continually rallied cast and crew to support her various political causes, sending most of us scuttling ignobly from the theater after a performance before we could be caught and harangued. For the sake of peace, many signed their names to pieces of paper they didn't even bother to read until it seemed we had joined a national strike and were expected to close the show and carry a large board branded with the words, THE CAST OF "DESIGN FOR LIVING" PROTEST, etc. We refused. Vanessa was not amused and stepped up her formidable recruiting campaign.

Secret meetings were held all over the theater and we managed to displace her as our Equity representative. The press was interested, as always, in a dispute and I was asked to tell all by a number of papers. I declined for the simple reason that Vanessa terrified the hell out of me and she's a very tall girl. I did not want to be chastised by an angry Trotskyist. Besides, I wanted her to go off and march and leave me a chance to play Gilda. Politics didn't come into it. It might be my last chance to show London what a talented actress I was. Each day my hopes were dashed, just as almost every week I was told Vanessa would be too late arriving and I would prepare to go on. This is a very nervewracking situation in the theater. I would shoot down to her dressing room, make up and dress for Gilda, add wig and hit the stage five minutes before curtain, only to be told that Vanessa had arrived and I wouldn't be playing the part. Not very good for morale.

I took it for a few months, my nerves shattered, until one matinee she did it again and I blew. I refused to get off the stage and so did she. There could have been a nasty scene if it hadn't been for my good manners: I told her she was a selfish bitch and walked off to complain to the other two stars who shook their heads sympathetically but dodged the ethical point involved. I called my agent and told him I was walking. He told me that wasn't very professional, and I asked him to define "professional" with regard to Vanessa. He told me to shut up and get on with the work, as the rest of the cast did. So I stopped packing and held on. But after that, I decided that the sooner the thing was over, the happier I'd be. After the public had satisfied their curiosity to see a real live political firecracker on stage, the figures dropped and the audience dwindled. *Design for Living* was over and so was my desire to walk the boards again. I decided that a once-very-promising career had finally reached the point of no return.

27

I DECIDED I'd do us all a favor by moving out of England to France, where I could be spared a fate worse than death, bankruptcy, for no matter how much I earned as an actress, the earnings were lumped together with my alimony from Finchy and I came out holding a third of it. Our dear surrogate father and guardian angel had been wonderfully generous, but being in effect a kept woman sat heavily on me. I'd always been to some extent "a kept woman," by my father, by Finchy, and now by this kind man. I decided to try and make a go of it on my own. Out of England I'd have my alimony in toto and that would keep us all very well, while I thought of what to do with my life. I approached the children with the plan and offered them the alternative, that they stay in England while I wander forth on foreign soil, a stranger in a new land, and try to figure out what the last ten years had been all about and where I would go from here. They decided to come with me.

It wasn't easy explaining to our dear friend that the time had come for me to make a major move and it's understandable that he felt I was betraying him by leaving, even though my motives sprang from courage rather than a better deal down the road. I wanted to work, to be free, and to be independent. I hadn't realized that all these things, so normal in the United States and even in England, were treated in France with great suspicion; I didn't know that until I got there.

It took me twenty-four hours to realize that the South of France was not the vibrating artistic cauldron I'd always envisaged. Graham Greene had an apartment in Antibes, yes, but he worked there intensely and alone after gathering his material from the real world elsewhere. There were painters and other writers and composers dotted around the hills, but they too worked in isolation. Mostly the Paradise Coast was populated with retired millionaires and active dealers on the make, and worst of all, over 70 percent of the residents in and around Cannes were pushing eighty years old. The glamorous *croisette* along the sea front looked like the planet of the geriatrics. We'd landed in one of the dead ends of the earth—I'd heard it called "a sunny place for shady people," and I couldn't clap my hands and say it's all been a terrible mistake and let's go to Paris or New York. Looked like I'd done it again. Frankly, I damned the day I'd ever divorced Finchy. I should have sweated it out and waited for him to grow up.

I frequently sat staring into the fire, wondering if the world had died and someone had forgotten to tell me. The children took to the television and from it gained the rudiments of the French language. In a very few months, they were fluent in it, while I wondered if I wasn't too old to try communicating at all, never mind in what language. I played records for myself until I could see through them, and huddled under my books in bed, destroyed.

At the beginning of our second month, no allowance arrived and from then on so it stayed for eight months. I sold everything I owned, including the well-earned string of pearls from Dibdin. I knew there would be a time for them to pay me back. In my protests of admiration of Peter Finch to impressionable people, I tried not to sound false, but the fact was that Finchy had stopped the alimony. A couple of old men propositioned me, suggesting bank accounts and other rewards for pleasure given, but it seemed to me I was a little old for the oldest profession, although I toyed with the idea. I tentatively asked for loans from attentive males, who laughed and said I could have everything if I'd give myself. How I longed to be a man and go out and scrub floors or drive a truck, anything than hump for money. There seemed only one thing to do.

I had poor old Finchy arrested in Jamaica on his banana plantation. He was put up in front of a judge who told him not to be naughty and pay up. With tradesmen hammering at the door each morning at six for their settlements, I didn't feel too bad about it. What on earth, I wondered, did he expect the children to live on. Goldfish?

Whether my demand through the courts persuaded Finchy to run for California and back into pictures, I'll never know, but to Hollywood he went and started his second-to-last picture, *Raid on Entebbe,* following it immediately with *Network*. Once again, mutual friends relayed news to me about him. It seemed he was on the wagon, living the life of a family man before, during and after his work and was quite a different man from the one I'd loved and married. Perhaps he had changed, after all. He was heard to say, "They're killing me, mate!" but I never knew if he referred to the black man behind his shoulder or to too much work.

After a bone-breaking promotional tour for *Network,* he appeared for a conference at the Beverly Hills Hotel to talk about the movie and the superb notices he'd received for his performance. Critics seemed certain he'd get the Academy Award for his portrayal of Howard Beale. Finchy had already applied for papers to become an American citizen and declared that his days as a rover were over. At last he was to settle down, but that demon who'd laid out his path, again thwarted him and took his life at his highest hour.

They buried him in Forest Lawn, a few bushes away from Cecil B. DeMille and next to Marion Davies. We haven't been to see the grave and I wonder what music plays to him there. I also wonder if Finchy, in his own mysterious fashion, meant it, when he said, with such feeling, in his last picture show:

"I've had enough and I'm not going to take any more!"